LARRY MATHIS
AND TODD DUFEK

TOOLS
OF THE
CROSS

WALKING WITH THE
MASTER CARPENTER

NEW YORK

TOOLS OF THE CROSS
WALKING WITH THE MASTER CARPENTER

LARRY MATHIS AND TODD DUFEK

ISBN 978-1-60037-735-8 Paperback
ISBN 978-1-60037-513-2 EPub Version
Library of Congress Control Number: 2009940761

Published by:

MORGAN JAMES PUBLISHING
The Entrepreneurial Publisher
5 Penn Plaza, 23rd Floor
New York City, New York 10001
(212) 655-5470 Office
(516) 908-4496 Fax
www.MorganJamesPublishing.com

Cover Design by:
Rachel Lopez
rachel@r2cdesign.com

Interior Design by:
Bonnie Bushman
bbushman@bresnan.net

In an effort to support local communities, raise awareness and funds, Morgan James Publishing donates one percent of all book sales for the life of each book to Habitat for Humanity.
Get involved today, visit
www.HelpHabitatForHumanity.org.

Ephesians 2:10

For we are his ***workmanship***, created in Christ Jesus for good works which God prepared beforehand that we should walk (emphasis added) in them.

Galatians 5:22–26

But the fruit of the Spirit is love, joy, peace, patience, kindness, goodness, faithfulness, gentleness, self-control; against such things there is no law. And those who belong to Christ Jesus have crucified the flesh with its passions and desires. If we live by the Spirit, let us also ***walk*** by the Spirit.

DEDICATION

This book is dedicated to Kim Schmidt.

On August 2, 2009 God called his servant Kim Schmidt home. For 12 years Kim served as the Executive Director of With Child, Ltd., a faith-based crisis pregnancy center in Phoenix, Arizona. Kim was a devoted wife to her husband Marc and mother to her four children. She dedicated her life to her Lord, her family and countless young women in crisis. She was God's special gift to With Child and to everyone she came in contact with; her smile and laugh will be remembered by all who knew her.

Kim phoned us many times with the news of an unborn baby saved from abortion or a life reborn through Jesus Christ. Or she would call to tell us about an anxious couple who had just taken their newly adopted baby home from the hospital who had sought her advice.

Kim gave so much of herself to benefit the lives of others and she never asked for anything in return. We can think of no one we have ever known who has done so much for so many people without a shred of a selfish motive. And as the song says, the many sacrifices she made, "they were unnoticed on the earth, in heaven now proclaimed!"

In the pages ahead we examine why God chose the profession of carpentry for his son and wonder why he has tarried so long to return. Perhaps part of the reason is that Jesus needed his skill as a craftsman, and enough time to build the many chests needed to hold all of the treasures he had in store for Kim in heaven. All who knew her will miss her here on earth, but for those of us who have hope in Jesus Christ, we will see her again one day in eternity.

ACKNOWLEDGEMENTS

This book would not have been possible without all the dedicated people at Morgan James Publishing. A special thanks to David L. Hancock, founder of Morgan James Publishing who believed in the unique perspective this tome has to offer and whose enthusiasm about its message fueled the desire to complete it. Our appreciation also goes to Margo Toulouse who worked with us from start to finish on this book helping us reach the goal of completion with the best possible outcome. Furthermore we want to thank ShellyWithem for her superior editing skills.

Of course, we would especially like to thank our wives and children who were so patient and encouraging during the entire process of putting this book together. Further, we would like to express our appreciation to our pastors past and present including: Jay Letey, Larry Wright, Randy Murphy, Skip Ast, John Politan and Kent DelHousaye. We also want to thank all of those people that took the time to write the testimonies that appear in this book as well as the authors of those who provided testimonies that do not appear in this work.

Finally, we must acknowledge our Savior and Lord, Jesus Christ. As a result of writing this book we appreciate even more fully the depth of his sacrifice. It is our hope that anyone who reads this book will come to the very same conclusion: the Son of Man's love for each one of us is beyond description. And something we can only thank him adequately for when we see him face to face.

Larry Mathis

Todd Dufek

ABOUT THE COVER

As authors, the publishing company gave us more than one option for the cover of this book. We chose the one we did because, like the unfinished heart being carved into the workbench, as long as we walk this earth God is continually working on our hearts.

PURPOSE OF THE BOOK

The purpose of this book is to help Christians become fully devoted disciples of Christ by learning to master the tools that Jesus used until he fulfilled his purpose on the cross.

Christ tells us in Matthew 16:24 that as Christians we are to "…take up our cross daily and follow him." Along with this command, God's Word admonishes us to become "…transformed into his likeness," 2 Corinthians 3:18. This transformation requires us to pick up the spiritual "tools" that Christ used and employ them daily in our own lives. And in so doing, become more like him.

This work also serves a powerful secondary purpose, providing a fresh insight into Christ's working life, ministry and crucifixion that will forever change your relationship with him. One that will lead to a new appreciation for what he faced in the years before his ministry began, and how it made the choice to lay down his life for each one of us even more harrowing.

Finally, the proper and consistent use of the *Tools of the Cross* is essential to becoming fully devoted followers of Christ. For just as a master carpenter expects his apprentice to use and become skilled with the tools of his trade, Jesus expects us to use these tools of Christianity each day.

TABLE OF CONTENTS

PREFACE

I was scheduled to instruct an adult Sunday school class on stewardship; the intent being to teach financial stewardship, a good fit with my profession as a CERTIFIED FINANCIAL PLANNER™, professional. However, as I studied scripture in preparation for the lesson I began to think about the various aspects of our lives that God has entrusted to us as stewards: our time, talents, children, the gospel, work, etc.

As part of the introduction to this lesson I was teaching on the "stewardship of our work" and quoted a verse from Colossians 3:23 that states, "Whatever you do, work at it with all your heart, as working for the Lord…" In other words, as followers of Christ, we should approach each task with the enthusiasm and pride that would be pleasing to God himself.

As an illustration of the verse I used the example of my brother-in-law Gary, a master carpenter and cabinet builder by trade, who came out to Phoenix from Iowa to build a shed next to my home. As I related to the class about how interesting and inspiring it was to watch a master carpenter apply his considerable skills to a project, I thought of Jesus and that he, too, was a worker of wood. I wondered what the "finished work" of Jesus must have looked like; the detail and the perfection of his carpentry must have been extraordinary.

The next hour in the church service, Skip Ast, a visiting pastor, was teaching on prayer. As he was speaking I contemplated what Jesus' prayer life was really like. Christ gave us insight into this aspect of his life during the agony that he experienced in Gethsemane as recounted in the gospels. And though Jesus taught us how to pray by answering a disciple's question about prayer, I began to feel that his prayer life must have been deeper and far more passionate than even the Bible tells us.

How did I come to this conclusion? Through "sanctified guessing" (my pastor John Politan's term) or from looking prayerfully at Scripture and drawing logical conclusions based on the evidence. For example, as a carpenter, Jesus was forced to face the reality of why he was here daily because, as you will see, *he used the same tools to make a living that were used to crucify him.* And thereby provide us with the means to salvation and eternal life with the Father.

As I sat listening to the sermon, questions came to mind: As a man, would Jesus have had the same concerns as us despite his impending crucifixion? Did he pray prior to Gethsemane to have "…this cup be taken from" him? My thoughts then turned to Luke 22:42 when Jesus' sweat was as blood in Gethsemane. He prayed, "Nevertheless, not my will, but yours be done."

The questions continued. Was that one prayer all he needed to be freed from the concern of separation from the Father or had he prayed it many times? Was it only as the time of his death drew near that sheer trepidation overran him (despite being reminded of his impending death by the physical tools, the hammer, nails and wood he used each and every day as a carpenter)?

As I thought more about these queries regarding Jesus' prayer life and the tools he used in his profession as symbols of his crucifixion, I remembered Jesus' remarks throughout the gospels that, "I and the Father are one." He also said in John 14:7, "If you really knew me, you would know my Father as well." Clearly, his ability to cope with daily employing the tools that would be used to bring about his death was in large part due to the nature of his relationship with God the Father.

As I continued to wonder about these things weeks after the service was over, four points became clear. These four concepts need to be kept in mind as you read this work:

1. As the son of a carpenter and as a carpenter himself, Jesus was surrounded by the literal "tools of the cross", the wood, hammer and nails, since early childhood. He was reminded every day of his purpose on earth. But only on one occasion, as illustrated in scripture, did he show any genuine concern about the coming crucifixion. Instead, he spoke often of it without any concern whatsoever.

2. Jesus carried a literal cross to Calvary and reminds us in Luke 9:23 that "If anyone would come after me, let him deny himself and take up his cross daily and follow me." The spiritual tools we will examine later require this choice each day and repeatedly. In other words, our faith takes practice to master and must be constantly supported by prayer.

3. Jesus continually reminds us that he, "…and the Father are one," (John 10:30). In all of eternity prior to the cross and in all eternity after his crucifixion, Jesus and the Father were and are, *never separated.*

4. Jesus was both God and man while here on earth. He faced the same fears and concerns, embraced the same joys and pains that all of us as modern believers must deal with each day. And that makes what he coped with in his daily life, and what he overcame in Gethsemane, as well as on the streets of Jerusalem, that much more awesome and unfathomable.

While considering the last point, it is essential to note that while praying in Gethsemane at one moment Jesus is sweating drops of blood as he is overwhelmed with anguish. Then immediately after he prays to the Father and says, "Not my will, but your will be done," he gets up and walks over to the disciples. "Why are you sleeping?" He seems to ask in disbelief, "Don't you know my time has come?" (Mark 14).

At this moment it seems as though his entire countenance changed from a toxic mixture of paralyzing fear and impending doom to that of peace, determination and rock solid commitment to fulfill his purpose. It's as if he's saying, "Come on guys let's go! It's time to get this done! I have nothing to worry about because my faith is in the Father."

Finally, it is here in Gethsemane where the spiritual tools of love, trust and obedience are so visibly and powerfully demonstrated. It is from this point forward that Jesus' ministry begins to fulfill its ultimate purpose: the road to and sacrifice upon the cross.

When you stop and think about it, this is exactly what God asks of us as his modern day disciples. These are the foundational, spiritual *Tools of the Cross*. For it is upon love, trust and obedience, that all other spiritual tools are based. We are told by Jesus himself that we must love others as we love ourselves and to "trust and obey," not "trust, *understand* and obey."

Finally, my hope is that by reading this short, yet powerful work, you will allow God to cultivate these "spiritual tools" in your heart. Also, that you would come to realize more fully what Jesus Christ had to come to grips with during his days as a carpenter, as well as appreciate more fully what he endured on the road to as well as upon the cross. And in the end, find your focus on the glory, grace and salvation that are yours because of his sacrifice.

Larry Mathis

When Larry said he had an idea for a Christian book and explained what he had in mind, I was intellectually and spiritually flabbergasted. So much so that I asked the most mature Christians I knew, including an elder at my church, if they had ever considered the fact that Jesus used the same tools each day as a carpenter that were employed to take his life. It came as no surprise that none of them had ever considered it. Nor had they heard of anyone—pastor, mentor, friend—ever make mention of the idea.

I quickly jumped on the Internet to see if anyone anywhere had ever contemplated the concepts we are about to share in the pages ahead. The only reference I could find-and it is related only to the ideas shared in this book about Christ being a carpenter-were a few articles authored by pastors and theologians explaining that our Savior's choice of a profession was no accident. But that it was a choice clearly made by God for several reasons, many of which overlap the conclusions Larry shares in the first chapter.

Taking on the task of co-writing a book such as this has been a humbling experience. Yes, I have been fortunate enough to have published a short book on a specific sport and the Christian faith. But like those before me who have been called to a task for him, I feel that God could have chosen someone with more skill, a greater network in the community of Christian writers, and typing skills to match (or at least far better ones!).

However, what I have learned in my own walk with Christ is that if you are being led to accomplish something worth doing for our Savior and know that you must depend more on God than you ever have to reach the goal, then he is in it. Nothing could be truer when it came to *"Tools of the Cross."*

If you have written a few pages on any topic you know that the process takes you on a journey. At the start your work is rough, unpolished and in need of fine-tuning. As a piece progresses, it becomes clearer. Ideas begin to crystallize, and in the end, hopefully something worth reading emerges.

In a very real way, writing allows an author to become creator, to have a part in the making of something worthwhile, both through the joys and frustrations experienced while in this role. And it helps those of us who love to string sentences together to appreciate how God must feel as he takes our rough-hewn faith in him and refines it through our life experiences so that it emerges as something more polished; a faith that more closely reflects the Creator Himself before he calls us to be with him for eternity.

It is my sincere wish that between now and that day that this short work will, along with the Holy Spirit's guidance, allow you to consider the ideas presented here with the result being a deepening of your faith in Jesus Christ or that you will find him as personal Savior. And finally, that you will be led to grow in ways you'd never pondered before this book found its way into your hands.

Todd R. Dufek

INTRODUCTION

What would your life be like, what would the daily grind of your existence come down to if you knew how and when you would die? More significantly, what would you do if you went to work each day the sun peeked over the horizon and used the very same tools to make a living that you knew were going to result in your own slow, unmerciful, humiliating, very public and agonizing death?

Out of our own sense of self-preservation, most of us would not want to be around the profession much less talk about it. We certainly would not touch or want to be intimate with the type of tools that would cause our own demise. The natural human reaction would be, in effect, to fear and avoid anything even remotely associated with the objects that would eventually end our existence on this planet.

We know a person who faced this fate and found joy and peace in the midst of it. We know a man who knew exactly how his life would end, yet called others to himself; loved and taught them like no one has before or since. We know a man who worked the wood that grew near his childhood home, fashioned it with an intimacy and unmatched pride using the same tools and type of lumber that would work in horrible concert to end his life.

His name is Jesus. And the wood, hammer and nails that he used daily to build furniture and other household wares were the very same implements and materials that he would allow a fallen world to bind him to a tree to free

1

humanity from sin. These, along with the traits that Christ possessed that allowed him to reach Calvary, are the *Tools of the Cross*.

Chapter One

WHY A CARPENTER?

"It amazes me how many Bible commentaries discuss Mary in great detail, but fail to mention Joseph. After all, Joseph was Jesus' earthly father; Jesus was known as 'the carpenter's son.'"

— Larry Mathis

Have you ever wondered why God the Father chose to have his son raised in the home of a carpenter? Knowing the culture of the time would probably result in Jesus becoming a carpenter himself, why didn't God choose a family that was headed by a farmer, shepherd, fisherman, doctor, soldier or more significantly, a military leader (each one of these professions was referred to in the gospels)?

After all, the Jews of the day were expecting a military leader that would break the shackles of control that were locked firmly in place by their Roman occupiers. They sought the type of figure that would literally ride in on a white horse and lead God's chosen people to a lopsided victory over a government that despised their ways as much as they misunderstood them.

Did God simply choose carpentry for his son, because Joseph, his earthly father, just *happened* to be a carpenter? Does God make haphazard decisions? Isn't there a purpose in everything he does?

If you could have walked the dusty path to his workshop…experienced the musty aroma of freshly cut lumber as Jesus planed the edge of a door… asked him point blank why he chose to work wood for a living, would he have said, "I am a carpenter, because my father was a carpenter, and his father was a carpenter and his father was a carpenter"?

As a result of studying Bible commentaries and examining what they have to say about the professions of the time period, I have read several different opinions as to why Jesus was a carpenter. And I have some of my own as well.

When we begin to carefully consider what God did in the book of Genesis, it seems only natural that his son had a carpenter's shop with all the tools necessary to create many types of wooden objects. God's workshop was the universe, and in it he crafted and created galaxies and hosts of stars and planets. God was in the creation business long before his son took it up in a far simpler form as a carpenter. And given what God had already done by bringing substance from nothingness, the profession of carpenter was a beautiful reflection of what the Father had accomplished long before the world began.

Another opinion is that as a carpenter Jesus could identify with the common people. And that as a worker of wood he could demonstrate the dignity of manual labor; that any profession can be carried out for "the glory of God." This view is quite common and expressed by a number of people whose sermons can be found on the Internet.

So were any of these options a part of God's purposes in selecting carpentry for his son? Though I do feel that carpentry is a very noble line of work, that Christ's chosen profession was no accident and that it mirrors God's attributes as Creator, I believe there was much more to it than that! Personally, I believe there could not have been a more perfect profession for the Son of God.

Why a carpenter then? While some answers have been provided, the complete picture of why Christ became a carpenter requires a closer examination of what it was like, what the Lord had to cope with as he worked wood nearly every day of his life.

Chapter Two

CHRIST AS CARPENTER, SAVIOR: THE DAY-TO-DAY REALITY

"The God on whom we rely knows what suffering is all about—not merely in the way that God knows everything, but by experience."

— D.A. Carson

Imagine that from the day you were born you are fully aware of when you will die and how, and the terrible emotional toll it will take on you before life slips from your battered and bruised body. Not only that, but you know every detail of the depth of the physical pain and anguish you will experience.

Visualize knowing not only exactly *how* you will die, but how unimaginably stressful it will be to survive—outlast each endless minute of the very public ordeal. Not to mention the fact that the salvation of countless humans; the entire weight of humanity rested on your ability, and your ability *alone*, to accomplish the task you came to complete.

Now consider that not only do you know the how, to the very detail and also the when, to the very second, but that every day of your life you will be surrounded by harbingers of the horrible manner of your death. Every single day as you reach your small, humble workshop you find your tools sitting there waiting silently for you on your workbench, yet screaming out your destiny. Each hour as you work you are reminded by them: the wood, hammer and the nails…you will feel the sins of man bearing relentlessly down upon every fiber of your being only to die in great pain and despair.

Not only that, but you will endure it in *complete* isolation. Ripped from a timeless bond that existed since before the creation of the universe, rent from a relationship that was more intimate than any human can possibly imagine, leaving you fully and utterly…*alone*.

The reality is that Christ knew what was going to happen to him long before his earthly father showed him the workbench and his first carpentry tool. He knew from the beginning of time exactly what he would have to face and overcome. He knew how many times he would be scourged, spat upon and struck in the face. He knew who his executioners would be before they were born, and daily reminders of his purpose came to him through the tools of his trade. Again, the literal "tools" of this carpenter's son were "*Tools of the Cross.*" How could he possibly have coped with this for so many years?

Was it mere coincidence that God put these implements around his son as he grew up? Was the adult Jesus allowed to daily use tools similar to the instruments that would cause his death on purpose so that he could be better prepared for what was to take place at Golgotha? He knew full well what a large nail, what a spike could do to the sturdiest piece of lumber. As he used his hammer to pound nails into wood, did he imagine it driving nails through his flesh to hold him to a tree?

We believe that God chose carpentry for his son so that every day of his life he would be confronted with his impending crucifixion; daily he would have to come face to face with the greatest fear any man could ever confront: death! God chose his son to be a carpenter so that in his humanity, i.e., as a man, Jesus would have to be totally dependent upon his Heavenly Father in order to have the strength to make it from day to day. And finally and most significantly, it helped him to fulfill his destiny on the cross of Calvary.

What is truly amazing, beyond comprehension really, is that it appears throughout scripture that Christ did not seem to be concerned about his impending death whatsoever. Though he knew full well the very number of blows the hammer would require to drive the nails through his hands and feet, the searing agony that would radiate through his body with each blow, not to mention the merciless beating and scourging he would suffer just prior to being nailed to the cross, Jesus never showed an ounce of concern whatsoever.

In fact, the first and only time Jesus showed any real "fear" in his entire life was not about the physical pain he would endure, but instead, it was about the separation from his Father in heaven that caused him to sweat blood in Gethsemane. As evening fell in that garden on the ominous night before his death, it was evident that Jesus would need to be "one with the Father." By choosing the profession of carpentry for Jesus, God surrounded and confronted his son with the cross of Calvary every day so that he would need to pray daily to be prepared for this exact moment in time.

Finally, what is vital for each believer to understand is that not only did Christ freely *allow* the physical tools of the cross to be used on him, but it required that he use an entirely different set of "spiritual tools" to reach Calvary. God's choice of carpentry was clearly no accident, but a choice that makes great sense when both "sets" of tools are considered. As noted earlier, it is the "spiritual tools" that we cannot only learn more about (see chapter six), but also apply to our Christian walk that will make us more effective and more devoted disciples and apprentices of the Master Carpenter.

Christ as Savior–The Day-to-Day Reality

There was another reality to the profession Jesus practiced for decades that probably occurred almost daily during the three brief years of his ministry. That was that those who heard him speak knew him only as a carpenter. And because of this simple profession, they were unable to see him in any other way—certainly not as the Savior or Messiah that they (the Jews) had been so desperately hoping for.

Can you imagine what it must have been like for Jesus to speak daily with those who desperately needed the love, forgiveness, grace and salvation he had to offer and for so many to fail to accept his message merely because of the trade he was born into? How the heart of Christ must have yearned, ached for those who knew him, those who saw him grow up to see beyond his former profession and realize he really was who he claimed to be (The Christ, The King of the Jews, The Messiah, The Light of the World, The Lamb of God…).

These two verses, Matthew 13:55 and Mark 6:2–3, are speaking of incidents when Jesus comes back to his hometown from Capernaum and is teaching in the synagogue. At first the people are amazed at Jesus' teaching, but then they ask, "Where did this man get this wisdom and miraculous powers? Isn't this the carpenter?" In these verses Jesus is clearly identified as the carpenter's son or "the carpenter." And in John 6:41–42 it says, "At this the Jews began to grumble about him because he said, 'I am the bread that came down from heaven.' They said, 'Is this not Jesus, the son of Joseph, whose father and mother we know?'" It is clear that the Jews that heard him speak were amazed and impressed by his teaching, yet their minds were unable to escape the reality that he was not only "just a carpenter," but the son of a carpenter they actually knew!

The profession that God chose for his son actually required those who heard Jesus to have a strong enough faith to be able to accept him as the Savior they had been promised. All because of the simple profession he practiced in their community was that of a carpenter.

The physical tools then have likely caused you to think differently about Christ's life, to more fully appreciate what he went through before and during his ministry. But there is more insight to be gained, more to learn from the days just before the literal tools carried out their cruel and vicious purpose.

Chapter Three

BEFORE THE TOOLS WERE USED

"It's not too late to restate and reestablish the obvious truth as the most important truth in your life—and to be caught up as never before in wonder over the love and grace of God."

—R.C. Sproul

In order to put the spiritual tools Christ utilized into proper perspective so that we can make effective use of them ourselves, it is important to understand the events that led up to Christ's death. In doing so, it will become clear that he had foreknowledge of his crucifixion, that as he used the tools of his trade in the decades prior to his ministry, he was forced to come to terms and cope with them as the symbols of his own destruction.

What made this doable? What can we learn from what Jesus did so that we can cope with the stressors and fears that invade our own lives?

Jesus Spoke of His Death on the Cross throughout the Gospels

Jesus knew what lay ahead not only in his every day life as a carpenter, but throughout his ministry. It's easy to draw such a conclusion by reading

9

Matthew 16:21–23 and 17:22–23. The scripture states that Jesus explained to his disciples that he must suffer many things at the hands of the elders, chief priests and teachers of the law, and that he must be killed and raised up on the third day. If he knew about his fate then, there's no reason to believe that he didn't know how his life would end before this point in his ministry.

Further, after Jesus finishes speaking to the Samaritan woman at the well in the fourth chapter of John's Gospel, she runs to her family and friends and says, "Come see a man who told me about all the things I ever did. Can this be the Christ?" (John 4:29). It is clear that Christ had the ability to look back as well as forward in time and that he knew, to the minutest detail, about his impending death.

It's very difficult to understand how Jesus could so easily talk about his crucifixion without becoming overwhelmed with worry, filled with anxiety and paralyzed by fear. Again, it is a reflection of his relationship with the Father and the spiritual tools he possessed.

Now let's return to the questions posed at the beginning of this chapter. First, what type of relationship did Jesus have with the Father that made dealing with the symbols (the physical tools) of his death, the constant reminders of what lie ahead, doable? Second, what can we learn by his example that will help us deal with the problems in our own lives?

Jesus Christ and the Father are One

We believe that Christ was able to cope with the daily reminders of his impending death because of the extraordinary closeness he had to his Father in heaven. In fact, he spoke of this relationship by frequently saying that they were "one" to the exclusion of any worry or fear. Evidence of the extraordinary relationship between the heavenly Father and his son was obvious in the only word picture we have of our Savior prior to his baptism.

In the second chapter of Luke, Mary and Joseph are returning to Nazareth from Jerusalem after celebrating the Passover. At this time Jesus was just

12-years-old. As you may recall, Jesus stayed behind in Jerusalem and his parents were unaware that he had done so.

Luke 2:46 says that when his parents returned to Jerusalem they found him in the temple courts talking with the teachers. Luke goes on to say that these men of wisdom were amazed at his understanding. When his frantic parents finally found him, his mother said, "Son, why are you treating us like this? Your father and I have been anxiously searching for you. " Jesus said, "Why were you searching for me? Didn't you know that I had to be in my Father's house?"

In John 8:42 Jesus says it was his Father who sent him. In John 5:30 he states, "By myself I can do nothing; I judge only as I hear, and my judgment is just, for I seek not to please myself but *him who sent me* (emphasis added)."

In John 8:13–18 Jesus is talking to the Pharisees who are arguing that Jesus' testimony about himself is not valid, because the Law requires two witnesses. Jesus tells them, "…I am not alone. I stand with the Father who sent me." He then goes on to say in John 8:19, "…If you knew me you would know my Father also." Finally in the first chapter of John it says, "In the beginning was the Word, and the Word was with God, and the Word was God. He was with God in the beginning."

The second question is: What can we learn from what Jesus did so that we can cope with the stressors and fears that invade our modern lives? To paraphrase Oswald Chambers' writings in his classic devotional, *My Utmost for His Highest*, we need to strive for the closeness with the Father that Jesus experienced by becoming as "haunted by God" as a child is "haunted by his mother."

Let us explain. In an Internet version of the book at http://www.rbc. org/utmost/index.php in a daily devotional entitled, "WHAT ARE YOU HAUNTED BY" dated June 2nd, Chambers says, "A child's consciousness is so mother-haunted that although the child is not consciously thinking of its mother, yet when calamity arises, the relationship that abides is that of the mother. So we are to live and move and have our being in God, to look at everything in relation to God, because the abiding consciousness of God pushes itself to the front all the time.

"If we are haunted by God, nothing else can get in, no cares, no tribulation, no anxieties. We see now why Our Lord so emphasized the sin of worry. How can we dare be so utterly unbelieving when God is round about us? To be haunted by God is to have an effective barricade against all the onslaughts of the enemy.

"'His soul shall dwell at ease.' In tribulation, misunderstanding, slander, in the midst of all these things, if our life is hid with Christ in God, he will keep us at ease. We rob ourselves of the marvelous revelation of this abiding companionship of God. 'God is our Refuge' nothing can come through that shelter."

What the author is saying here is to keep your focus on God. For just as we are encouraged to "pray continually" (1 Thessalonians 5:17) or without ceasing, we need to constantly be turning to our Lord for help, to be in dialogue with him as much as possible.

On the most basic psychological level, it is helpful to verbalize and talk about your problems with another human being for many more reasons than can be detailed here. Doesn't it make sense then to be in constant contact with a God who loves you more than you can possibly imagine?

It may sound simplistic and trite, but we would find our lives far less stressful if we prayed more, worried less, and turned to God for help on not just a daily, but hourly and often moment-to-moment basis. Something Jesus must have done many times during and prior to allowing the tools of his trade to be used on himself.

Chapter Four

CHRIST ALLOWED THE TOOLS TO BE APPLIED

"Jesus doesn't just feel forsaken; He is forsaken. In an unfathomable mystery, at that moment, as God's wrath is poured upon him as the substitute for our sin, Jesus is rejected by God. His Father turns his face away from him. It isn't a deceptive feeling; it's reality."

— C.J. Mahaney

Of course, the time came for the literal *Tools of the Cross* to be applied, or Christ to die for the sins of mankind. But before that event took place, Jesus made it clear by example that we must carry our cross as he did. In Luke 14:27 he says, "And anyone who does not carry his cross and follow me cannot be my disciple."

So what is the cost of being a disciple of Jesus the Christ? The cost is dying to self. That is, we must be willing to live life on God's terms, not our own. The cost is the willingness to carry our burdens and at the same time glorify God by the way we use the spiritual *Tools of the Cross*.

The best example of carrying one's cross, utilizing the spiritual tools *and* allowing the literal *Tools of the Cross* to be applied took place two millennia ago...on a windswept, lonely, rock covered out cropping just outside the walls of Jerusalem. Christ, battered and bloody, reaches his final destination: the place where he will give his life away.

Physically beaten, bloodied, spent beyond exhaustion and emotionally shattered, he drops his cross with a thud and crumbles to the ground, his crown of thorns tearing at the flesh around the top of his head. After enduring unrelenting public humiliation and hours of physical agony, he lays groaning on the cold, hard ground. In the sky overhead black, water-laden clouds are gathering like an angry mob, light is growing dimmer, and the scent of rain is on the gathering wind.

Before Jesus has a moment to try and orient himself, wood rumbles over the ground like distant thunder as men around him straighten the roughhewn cross beside the Lord and motion for the Son of God to take his place. He does so without hesitation, drawing the last vestiges of strength to lay his body and limbs upon the cross so that the nails, the spikes, can be driven home. And the suffering he knows he must endure can begin so that it can end in salvation of mankind.

Now, if this were some ordinary criminal that was part of a band of thieves, he might have recruited those closest to him to attempt a rescue before being so cruelly pinned to beams of wood. Perhaps he would have been belligerent, unruly and uncooperative to buy himself more time. He would look for ways to stall, to prevent his suffering and death so that help could arrive. Even in the midst of his guilt and exhaustion he would look for a way out.

In the Son of God was a man who had the unbridled strength of an incomprehensible God, the Creator of the universe and ruler of countless angels at his disposal. Yet, he called out for *nothing*…His primary focus was forgiving those whose actions put him where he now suffered, bearing all of our sins so that we might live.

In the simplest of terms, Jesus permitted the tools he had known all of his life to take his. And on top of all of this, he was guilty of nothing and innocent of all charges brought against him. This application of the "justice" and false accusations he had experienced would be hard for any man to take without defending himself, but Christ didn't utter a word in defense.

He willingly carried the horrendous burden of his own cross. He allowed a hand full of humans to use those objects he knew so well from every day experience; the literal *Tools of the Cross* to pierce his hands and feet until the physical cost of what he went through took his life. In short, he allowed human injustice by the cruelest means that resulted in his merciless death, the only death that could bring eternal life to those who know him as Lord and Savior.

The Anguish of Christ

What makes this far more difficult for any human to fully understand is that this event in Christ's life was more than a sacrifice for our sins. It meant that Jesus would have to experience something so foreign, something so far beyond the realm of his existence that to think of it created the only "fear" it appears he ever felt. This event, as noted earlier, was the breaking of an eternal bond with his Father. A relationship so tied up in the mysteries of time and space that it is more than any human can wrap his mind around.

God knew that his son would have to be one with him or else he would end up focusing on his crucifixion. Toward that end, Jesus' prayer life must have been truly amazing. Since we are admonished in 1 Thessalonians 5:17 to "…pray without ceasing," this is surely what Christ did during nearly every waking moment of his life both before and during his brief ministry. In fact, it was his prayer life that gave him the strength to overcome seeing the symbols of his death every day.

In summary, by allowing the actual *Tools of the Cross* to be applied and dying for our sins, Christ demonstrated the spiritual tool of love first and foremost. The tools of obedience and trust, fulfilling his purpose by obeying God, and at the same time trusting his Father for the strength to carry it out, were the second and third tools that Jesus used.

Though it pales in significance with Christ's suffering, every one of us who knows Jesus as personal Savior have our own stories of personal anguish that demonstrate this same love, obedience and trust, the three most significant spiritual *Tools of the Cross*. That includes the authors of this book.

Larry's Anguish

Have you ever faced such a significant event that every time you thought about it you broke out in a cold sweat and were hit by a crashing wave of anxiety? Nearly everyone has. Perhaps before your college finals or board exams? Or perhaps you can recall a similar feeling if your mother ever said, "Wait until your father gets home!" We've all had moments that filled us with fear on one level or another.

I remember the exact moment when I confronted feelings like this that were overwhelming. It was the afternoon that I fully came to the realization that I was going to die, that I would cease to exist. Keep in mind as you read the story below that I did not know Jesus Christ as my personal Savior at the time.

I was in my hometown of Phoenix, Arizona driving on I-17, the only major interstate highway at the time. From a pastel blue sky that held only a few fluffy clouds the sunlight splashed across the desert as the car carried me comfortably through the city toward my destination. As I listened to the group Kansas' song "Dust in the Wind" I navigated a corner of the freeway known as the Durango Curve.

All of the sudden, as if I'd been slapped hard across the face, I realized that the lyrics of the song were true, "*All we are is dust in the wind.*" In the grand scheme of things, within the vast expanse of the universe, I realized that I was nothing—no more than a speck of dust!

At that exact moment, for the first time in my life, I came to the hard realization that some day I would die and I would be dead *forever*! What was a comfortable, enjoyable trip across the desert turned nightmarish. I become physically sick to my stomach. I broke out in a cold sweat. I trembled all over.

All I could think about was that I was going to die. My existence would end and that was it! That day stretched into four long years where I lived nearly every day steeped in a brew of anxiety, fearing my demise.

I want you to know I wasn't actually afraid of the event itself or the process of dying. I was acutely afraid of being dead. My thoughts of death were simple: death would come and I would experience nothingness. I wasn't afraid of hell and wasn't sure if there was a god or heaven. My fear was that there was an eternity filled with nothingness!

During the four-year period following that fear-filled afternoon, the nights were the worst. I would do just about anything to keep from going to sleep. I knew that if I went to bed my imagination would run wild with thoughts of dying and the vast nothingness that was waiting for me. The panic attacks would kick in, followed by trembling, sweating, rapid heartbeat, a stomachache and overwhelming fear. Fear that I compare to that of a soldier facing death in battle.

Why was I afraid? Because I knew that death was coming. It was inevitable, inescapable and closing in on me with each passing second. I didn't know when I would die and it really didn't matter. Whether I lived another 8 hours, 8 days, 80 years, or 800 years, for that matter, someday I was going to die and be dead forever! Forever is forever—an amount of time as huge and measureless as eternity.

There was nothing I could do to alleviate this fear, nowhere I could hide and there was no way to escape. It was the equivalent of carrying a mental jail cell around with me. In a very small way perhaps it was possible that God was allowing me to experience the same anguish that his son felt the night before his death in Gethsemane. A fear and trembling that comes when facing death without the presence of the Father.

In time I would hear the Good News of the Gospel of Jesus Christ. And there came a day of salvation when I realized I had sinned, could not be a child of God because of it, and accepted Christ as my personal Savior. In doing so, my fears of nothingness and death were replaced by trust in a loving God and eternal life in heaven. The anxiety and fear I'd grappled with for years melted away immediately! I didn't know it at the time, but I'd barely gotten my hands on the two remarkable tools of trust and obedience, but the change was unmistakable. I would never be the same again.

Todd's Anguish

In 1986 the world as I knew it collapsed. Everything I'd set my sights on, the goals I hoped to achieve and one of the people I wanted most to share it with, were gone within months of one another. Between my undergraduate work in Behavioral Sciences and earning a Masters Degree in Social Work, I'd spent more than half a decade working toward my desire to be a counselor and help people. However, four years into my profession I found out it wasn't for me.

And about the time I called it quits, my father, whom I admired greatly, died suddenly and without warning. In fact, I was the first of the five children to receive the call no one wants to get from a tearful, shaken mother; "Todd, your father just died of a massive heart attack…" There would be no good byes.

A few months after these events I found myself back at my mother's home doing much needed repairs and touch ups on the exterior of the house. Despite being a Christian for most of my life and thoroughly convinced that everything that happens has a purpose, I had a hard time believing it. I had to force myself to trust the God I'd always had faith in. After all, the job I'd studied and trained so hard for was gone…and I would never see my dad again.

What purpose could such grief, having to endure the loss of both my father and profession at the same time possibly serve? Where was the God that promised he'd never leave me?

I took these questions before God, along with my anger, grief and despair, and with paper and pen, filled notebooks with prose that turned into poetry. Even before these events occurred, God had orchestrated a miracle:

allowing me to attend a writer's conference in the Northwest that cost nearly $1,000.00 when I was living paycheck to paycheck. Long after these events I took a writing course via correspondence that took two years to complete, but gave me the basics of writing stories as well as the mechanics of the craft. I had obediently walked through the literary doors that God had opened and worked hard to hone a gift I never knew I had.

That conference and surviving those watershed events left me with a love of writing and the desire to publish a book that honored God, shared the gospel, and provided believers and non-believers with a reason to both deepen their faith and find it, respectively. That new desire, that journey began with the publication of a book in 2007 entitled, *Cypress Tree Odyssey: Making Sense of Trials and Tests On and Off the Golf Course* (Amazon.com) and continues with the printing of this one. In the simplest of terms, God knew what he was doing all along and figured that my faith needing growing at the same time.

Had the Lord I trusted for years abandoned me in the middle of my worst life crisis? Not for a second! He was there all the while, but was difficult to find with a heart so burdened with grief and despair. And in time, with the help of family, friends, and God's guidance, I found another profession I enjoy that has given me time to do what I love most: write Christian books.

Christ's love, our obedience and trust were powerful spiritual tools in both of our lives. And when combined with the others that lie ahead, you will find your faith stronger and your walk with Christ deeper. But first, it is important for both the Christian and non-Christian to understand that a separation exists between God and those who do not accept Christ. And that sin affects the spiritual walk of believers as well.

Chapter Five

OUR SEPARATION FROM THE FATHER

"It is a stark, unforgiving reality that those who do not accept Christ will one day be on the outside looking in. Find themselves outside God's kingdom because sin has caused separation from the Father—a God that loves non-believers more than they can ever imagine."

— Todd Dufek

As authors of a book such as this, we realize that it will find its way into the hands of Christians and non-Christians. And that both groups need to understand that sin affects the relationship between themselves and God. That is because in the case of Christians, it has a very real influence on how effective we are in the use of the spiritual tools that we have been entrusted with.

Recently my (Larry's) Sunday school class completed a six-week study on the subject of sin. To get started, those teaching the class asked the following question: How would you define sin to a non-believer? The answer? It's a transgression of God's moral law. More importantly, to the non-believer sin is what separates him or her from God. This separation is the result of committing sin and not accepting Christ as personal Savior.

The outcome is eternal separation from God and is what I feared when I first realized that I was going to die. As you recall, nothingness was what I feared most, even though what I should have feared was a real place called Hell with eternal punishment. Much worse than any definition of nothingness that I could ever imagine!

It is important to keep in mind here that sin is "positional" in that it defines our position with God as "saved" or "unsaved." For the non-believer, God's word tells us that sin is unforgiven and therefore sin is what separates him or her from God. This rift, this separation is not for hours, days or even centuries, but is for eternity!

How long is an eternity? Think of it this way (an example I heard on the radio): imagine a square block of cement that is 10 miles in every direction (10 miles wide, high and thick). Once every 10,000 years a sparrow finds its way to this massive block of cement and swipes its beak across a tiny portion of it. When enough 10,000 year time periods have passed and enough sparrows have landed to swipe their beaks across it (one time each) to turn this enormous block of cement to dust, this will be the beginning of eternity!

To be frank, the spiritual death we speak of is one that never ends. As the Bible says, "For the wages of sin is death, but the free gift of God is eternal life through Jesus Christ."

The class was also asked this question on the same topic during a subsequent class: How would you define sin for the believer? The conclusion we came to was that for the Christian, sin is anything that goes against the will of God or those principles taught in God's word. Of course, as noted, for non-believers sin goes unforgiven. But for Christians sin is forgiven and eternal life in heaven is theirs.

However, as believers even though our sin is forgiven, it can keep us from having a right relationship with God. When we sin and leave our sin unconfessed before him and possibly someone we sinned against, our relationship or our walk with God is hindered. In other words, if we don't confess our sin before the Father we cannot have the best or closest relationship possible with him. For the Christian sin is also "relational" in that it defines how good our relationship with God is at a particular point in time.

This type of sin is what affected my relationship with God after I came to Christ when I had un-confessed sin in regard to my hateful feelings toward my dad (see Larry's story under the "Tool of Forgiveness"). Although I was a believer and had been saved from a positional standpoint, my relationship with my Heavenly Father was strained due to the sin I still had in my life. In the simplest of terms, until I dealt with this sin, asked God's forgiveness and claimed his promise of it, I could not truly be in close fellowship with God the Father.

Interestingly, until God led me to forgive my dad, when asked about him I always referred to him as my *father*, not my *dad*. Once I forgave him and God relieved me of my pain and the guilt of unforgiveness, I was able to call him my *dad*.

Put another way, the believer has a relationship as well as fellowship or closeness to and with God. If a Christian confesses his sin to God regularly, asks for forgiveness and turns from sinful behavior that is unacceptable, he will stay close to God or be in fellowship with him. If sin remains un-confessed and the Christian unrepentant, he will lose the fellowship or closeness but still has a relationship with God. However, the fact that he has adopted us into his spiritual family can never be altered.

Let's simplify things by looking at this from inside a relationship between two people. If a father and son stay in consistent contact with one another, ask each other for forgiveness when they wrong each other, and work through any issues that come up, they can be said to have close fellowship as well as a good relationship between them.

However, if the son (the prodigal son, for example) decides he no longer wants to talk with his father for whatever reason, he loses his fellowship with his dad. But one thing cannot change; they will always be father and son—no matter what either says or does. So although they are still related physically, they may lack emotional or spiritual closeness. In the case of the prodigal son, it was when the son returned to his father in repentance, that the relationship was restored.

To conclude this chapter on how sin affects Christians and non-Christians, it is important for every believer to realize that there is still another set of tools that we can use as believers, and unfortunately, often do. They are the Tools of Sin or the Tools of Satan and they can and do affect the closeness of our relationship with the Father. Put another way, these are the tools of bitterness, hatred and selfishness to name just a few. For non-believers these are the tools that lead to spiritual death and, to be blunt, an eternity in hell.

—————————

At this point in the book we have discussed the difference between the believer and non-believer along with the eternal consequences of not accepting Christ as your Lord and Savior. If you are a non-believer and picked up this book because the title and content grabbed your attention (or were given this book by a Christian friend), and you would like to know more about this Jesus and accept him as your personal Savior, we would like to extend an invitation to do so right now and provide you with the means. We have done so in the back of this book. We encourage you to turn there now and read "Out of the Carpentry Shop" by Max Lucado and ask Christ into your life.

It is more important than any decision you'll ever make because it is the only one with eternal consequences. By doing so you will understand more fully what is being taught by this work and how it can be applied to your new and daily walk with Christ. After having carried out that step, we encourage you to find a solid, local Bible teaching church so that you can continue to grow as a Christian and enjoy the fellowship of other believers.

Finally, it would give us great joy to know that what you read in this book led you to make a decision for Christ. Please visit our web site at http://www.toolsofthecross.com and let us know about it using the "Contact Us" link on the home page. We'd like to get in touch with you and encourage you for taking such an important step.

As believers we have a choice to make; one as extreme as picking up our cross and following Christ or turning aside and seeking our own will. The choice we must make is whether or not to pick up destructive tools instead of those Christ gave us and allow them to affect our relationship with him. God wants us to use his tools; the polar opposite of the Tools of Sin.

Oftentimes as Christians we, without even realizing it, hold a spiritual tool in one hand and a sin tool in the other and make a snap decision, utilizing a Tool of Sin instead of those tools Christ entrusted to us. But that's part of the process. You cannot move toward mastery of the spiritual tools without making mistakes. After all, most of us have had more practice with sin tools than spiritual ones. And it takes time, effort and God's help to make the transition to those he wants us to employ.

The latter will be discussed in great detail in the next chapter, including how Jesus used them. And will include not only an appropriate scripture, but stories of how modern day believers have employed these tools to deepen their faith, walk closer with their Creator and become more devoted and effective disciples.

It's time, then, to open the door of the Lord's spiritual carpenter's shop, walk up to the work bench, and take a close, careful look at each tool. It's time to examine each one so that we can learn to walk more closely with the Master Carpenter.

Chapter Six

THE SPIRITUAL
TOOLS OF THE CROSS

"When we think of Christ's dying on the cross we are shown the lengths to which God's love goes in order to win us back to Himself. We would almost think that God loved us more than he loves his son. We cannot measure his love by any other standard. He is saying to us, 'I love you this much.'"

— Sinclair Ferguson

There was certainly a time when Joseph took Jesus with him to his workbench. One can only imagine the wonder in the boy's eyes when he strolled into his father's workshop for the first time, experienced the aroma of freshly cut wood and saw shavings strewn across the dirt floor. With eyes wide in awe his mouth probably fell open as he gazed at the many tools his father skillfully used to create wooden pieces of all shapes and sizes.

The Son of God probably watched his earthly father make countless items and received careful instructions on how to create each one so that his labor would end in a well-crafted wooden object. Christ undoubtedly learned what all workers of wood both ancient and modern know: every tool of the carpenter has a specific purpose.

Then came the day perhaps when Jesus was a teenager, when Joseph's son took the tools into his hands and began to create handcrafted, useful items through his own efforts, proudly carrying on the family profession of carpentry.

As a child of God, the time has come for you to pick up the tools from the Lord's spiritual workbench and take them into your heart and life. As a result, your relationship with our Lord will deepen. Your life will be an even more effective living testimony to others that you are indeed a Child of the King. And in the end, your example will hopefully lead them to accept Jesus as Savior; pick up the tools, and proudly carry on this extraordinary aspect of Christianity.

As noted earlier, the tools that Christ learned to use in his inherited profession of carpentry were the literal *Tools of the Cross*. Of course, the most important question for modern disciples is: *What are the spiritual Tools of the Cross that Jesus wants each one of his followers to practice with and become skilled at using?*

Before reading the answers to this question, I'd like you to think about something. As disciples of Christ we are called to follow and be like him. As Ephesians 5:1 succinctly points out, we are to "...Be imitators of God." When defined from the vantage point of a carpenter or craftsman, it is clear that we are to be our Lord's spiritual "apprentices," always walking with the Master Carpenter. That means, in this context at least, that we need to put the same spiritual tools to work for us that Jesus used.

Just as an airline pilot must rehearse the unexpected in a flight simulator in order to properly control an actual aircraft when dealing with the sudden forces of wind sheer. Or a surgeon doing an appendectomy needs to know exactly what to do if a patient abruptly goes into cardiac arrest—we need to be prepared, as Christ was, to use the appropriate tool when the situation presents itself.

Simply put, the only way to become better at using the spiritual tools is *practice*. And practice is hard. For Jesus, picking up the literal cross was difficult. In his humanness Christ required help carrying the beams, but he did pick them up. Sometimes our cross, i.e., a difficult life circumstance may become too heavy to bear. That is when we must hand our cross over to Christ. The same goes for the spiritual tools. We must be willing, with the Holy Spirit's help, to pick them up and try to master each one. But if a particular tool is too difficult to use, we need to hand it over to Christ so that he can help us with it.

All too often we use excuses like, "I just can't find time to pray" or perhaps, "Self-control is not something I'm good at." In short, there is no room for excuses for not using the tools as we walk through life with the Master Carpenter. God simply wants us to be more like him by using the tools Jesus did, and there is no way we can do that without confronting trials and suffering. And when we use a tool in their midst and it results in something as wonderful as our becoming more Christ-like, we are called to consider it all joy! (James 1:2-4)!

Another important thing to remember as you head into this area of personal application is that you cannot only practice using the tools now and grow closer to the Lord, but after reading all of them, we encourage you to examine the tools on the list that you've used in the past, how frequently they have been employed, and prayerfully observe where your strengths and weaknesses lie among those listed. In doing so, you can, like a journeyman carpenter, determine what tools you need to spend more time on in order to move closer to the mastery that God desires.

Further, through our prayer life we can go to the Lord and ask him for wisdom to show us what tools we need to use more often than the others. And just as importantly, how to use them in our unique spiritual walk. As his apprentices he will give us insight through the Holy Spirit and opportunities to improve our abilities with each one.

Likewise, it is important to realize that there are two types of spiritual "Power Tools." The first is suffering, oftentimes of an acute nature. Whether it manifests in the intense grief over the loss of a loved one or severe physical pain that results in an individual questioning his desire to live with or beyond it, nothing grows us more quickly spiritually; burns away all that is unnecessary apart from our relationship with Christ.

The second is not so much a "Power Tool," but rather how each one can be viewed. For example, one of the authors of this book was hanging a door in his house, needed to drive a long screw through a hinge and into the door frame, and asked his toddler-aged son if he would like to help. When the son arrived on the scene his eyes looked like saucers as he stared up in wonder at his dad and the gigantic door—at least from where he stood.

With anticipation holding his face captive, hands moving about in his pockets and feet shifting up, down and around like he needed to visit a bathroom or risk a potty accident, he stood squirming with delight not knowing what to do with himself. He was so excited simply because his father had asked for help with a job that seemed beyond his ability. But here was his dad inviting him to try.

Now alone and given a screw driver, the little man stood no chance of accomplishing the goal of helping with the project and pleasing his father. But when his dad handed him an electric drill and showed him how to use it, he took the tool slowly into his small hands, looked it over carefully, and smiled from ear to ear with delight.

His face positively beamed because his father had entrusted it into his care. Thrill was added to the delight when the son drove the screw home and accomplished what his dad had asked of him. It was as if the son was saying, "Wow!! Dad trusts me with this powerful tool, counted on me to use it correctly, and I did it!"

You've probably reached the conclusion before I could draw it…as God's children we too should be filled with joy when God entrusts us with a spiritual "Power Tool," it gives him great pleasure when we use it, and it is because of his strength and trust (like the author had in his son) that we can use it properly. And when we are confronted with an adult set of circumstances that cause us to respond with anger, pride and self-righteousness we can react instead by using the tools described below. As a result we are again made more into the likeness of Christ.

In summary, the only way we can move toward mastery of the spiritual *Tools of the Cross* is to be required to use them. We are not talking about being tempted by Satan, but what we are saying is that God allows circumstances into our lives that require us to pick up each tool and put it to use. In other words, when you find yourself in a trying situation in the future you no longer have to wonder what God is trying to teach you. Like a carpenter who needs to build a specific piece of furniture, just mentally review the tools and determine which one is right for the job.

Finally, to make this most important section of the book as beneficial as possible and life application of each spiritual tool simpler, a basic format will be followed. First, the spiritual tool will be identified, an appropriate "tool verse" or verses from scripture will be provided, and an example given from the gospels of how the Lord used it.

Next is a section entitled, "As his Apprentices" with verses that apply to modern day disciples followed by a short commentary examining the tool in the light of our current cultural climate. Finally, one or two present day believers will give his or her example(s) of how they or others they observed put the tool into practice in their lives. For a few of the tools, examples from the authors have been included.

The Spiritual *Tools of the Cross*

1. The Tool of LOVE

Tool Verses:

John 3:16 "For God so loved the world that he gave his one and only Son, so that whoever believes in him shall not perish but have everlasting life."

Romans 5:8 "But God demonstrates his own love for us in this: While we were still sinners, Christ died for us."

1 Corinthians 13:4–7 "Love is patient, love is kind. It does not envy, it does not boast, it is not proud. It is not rude, it is not self-seeking, it is not easily angered, it keeps no record of wrongs. Love does not delight in evil but rejoices with the truth. It always protects, always trusts, always hopes, always perseveres."

Luke 6:27–28 "But I tell you who hear me: Love your enemies, do good to those who hate you, bless those who curse you, pray for those who mistreat you."

The Master Carpenter's Use of the Tool:

Anyone the least bit familiar with Christ's life would probably agree that the most significant spiritual tool he used was love. And Christ lived it like Paul defined it in 1 Corinthians 13 above. Love is what Jesus taught, what his ministry was built on, and was the reason for his sacrifice. In the most basic Christian terms, love pursues sacrificing for others rather than gratifying self.

Jesus openly demonstrated his love for his disciples (despite their later betrayals), for those considered outcasts by the culture of his time, and for those with infirmities by his gentle and compassionate treatment of them. On top of all of this, he freely chose to bear the sins of the world so that every human being could find redemption, salvation and eternal life.

Dozens of examples of this love come to mind from biblical texts, but none more closely mirrors the sheer immensity of the Lord's love for us than what took place on a cross atop a desolate hill outside of Jerusalem. If laying down your life to save the life of another person is indicative of the strength of one's love and the moral character of the person making the sacrifice… how great is Christ's love for us given that he willingly handed himself over to be crucified and bore the sins of countless humans? "Immeasurable," "incalculable" and "inestimable" fall far short as descriptors.

As Sinclair Ferguson was quoted as saying to begin this chapter, "When we think of Christ's dying on the cross we are shown the lengths to which God's love goes in order to win us back to Himself. We would almost think that God loved us more than he loves his son. We cannot measure his love by any other standard. He is saying to us, 'I love you this much.'"

As His Apprentices:

John 13:34–35 "A new command I give you: Love one another. As I have loved you, so you must love one another. By this all men will know that you are my disciples, if you love one another."

Matthew 22:37–39 "Jesus replied: Love the Lord your God with all your heart and with all your soul and with all your mind. This is the first and greatest commandment. And the second is like it: Love your neighbor as yourself. All the Law and the Prophets hang on these two commandments."

John 15:12–13 "This is my commandment, that you love one another as I have loved you. Greater love has no one than this, that he lay down his life for his friends." (ESV)

Ephesians 5:1–2 "Therefore be imitators of God, as beloved children. And walk in love, as Christ loved us and gave himself up for us, a fragrant offering and sacrifice to God." (ESV)

Commentary:

Not only has American culture diluted the meaning of the word "love" like a drop of lemonade in the Atlantic ("I love my car," "I just love this dessert," etc.), the effort and time required to build a friendship or marriage based on biblical, sacrificial or servant love seems almost beyond us as a society. Why? It only takes a sociological glance to understand the reasons.

As scripture so wisely and forcefully points out, love does not seek its own way, it is patient and often calls for sacrifice, a desire to work through conflict over the long haul by leaving self-interest at the wayside—caring enough for another human being to hear the person out before trumpeting our own opinions. This just happens to be the opposite of what we as Americans are taught from birth to our dying day: needs are to be met instantly…if you want it you can have it. Even if you don't need it, marketing gurus will convince you that you can't live without it.

Even as Christians, it is very difficult to live outside the norms of what we call, "extreme instant gratification." That is, confusing "wants" for "needs" and buying or pursuing what we *think* will make us happy, through vehicles such as credit cards, sex, alcohol or other means. And many of us, the authors included, are guilty of bowing before the god of personal happiness rather than putting our needs, at least some of the time, second to those we have committed our lives and love to.

What we are saying is that what Christ did on Calvary was the purest, costliest, most selfless act of love ever committed by any human being. And that our society as a whole encourages us to meet our own needs swiftly and in excess. Love, as has been defined here, takes time, honorable effort backed up by consistent actions.

Todd will explain more clearly what we mean by the example below of two special Christians' use of the Tool of Love in his own life.

Example of a Believer's Use of the Tool (Todd):

I have walked the earth for over a half century, been a Christian for over 35 of those years, and during that time have carried out what most would consider unselfish acts of love that were a result of my relationship with Christ. But when I contemplated describing a personal example of the use of this tool, anything I've done fell far short of how two Christians powerfully demonstrated and used this tool to impact my life. Those two people? My parents Harry and Alice.

Having only been a dad for eight years at the time of this writing (I've been told repeatedly that these are the "easy years" when your child, "… still thinks you're cool"), I can tell you that there has been, for me at least, no other life circumstance that has called me to wholehearted selflessness, sacrifice and love.

In other words, like a bouquet of flowers purchased for the most precious occasion, your thoughts are preoccupied with what that little human requires to develop in every way. And what actions you need to carry out so that your child can have the greatest chance of blossoming into a Christ—centered, mature adult.

My parents brought five such "flowers" into the world and I was the last of those little bloomers. Not only did they instill Christian values in us by taking us to church and teaching us about God's love, they ran a family shoe business that was an example of caring and fairness in the two communities in which it thrived. To be a part of this family, I learned early on, was to be held in high-esteem by our neighborhood and community, a fact that made me immensely proud to be even the youngest of the brood.

How did my parents use the Tool of Love? Obviously, it's essential to look back and see how the instrument was used, and in this case, for the benefit of my siblings and me.

In short, my dad worked long hours in our family business to make it successful. My mother worked at his side to lessen expenses and used her considerable book keeping skills and kindness to grow the business into a successful one. Their daily use of the Tool of Love as reflected by their hard work to provide what their children needed apart from their personal desires and goals (a college education among them) were obvious. The use of this tool was evident over years of countless sacrifices that were as consistent as they were loving and personal to each one of their offspring.

To paraphrase a famous basketball player whom, when asked by a reporter if he felt he was a role model, scoffed, chuckled sarcastically and said with all the seriousness he could muster, "Moms and dads who go off to work every day and provide for their families are the real 'role models,' not me."

In my mom and dad were two loving, hard working, high school educated Christians who provided well for their children and continually sought God's will and wisdom in all they did for us. And with the passing of the decades along with their efforts and support, they put all five of us through college, each of us earning undergraduate diplomas, two earning master's degrees.

All of this from a loving mother partnered with a humble shoe repairman that worked on an estimated quarter of a million pairs of shoes, sending his offspring into the world to find success by adeptly using the Tool of Love and…a hammer and nails.

2. The Tool of FAITH/TRUST

Tool Verses:

John 14:12 "I tell you the truth, anyone who has faith in me will do what I have been doing. He will do even greater things than these…"

1 John 1:9 "If we confess our sins, he is faithful and just and will forgive us our sins and purify us from all unrighteousness."

Matthew 17:20 "He said to them, 'Because of your little faith. For truly, I say to you, if you have faith like a grain of a mustard seed, you will say to this mountain, 'Move from here to there,' and it will move; and nothing will be impossible for you.'" ESV

The Master Carpenter's Use of the Tool:

Our Lord used the spiritual tools of faith and trust across the length and breadth of his ministry, from the moment he stepped into the Jordan River to be baptized to when he ascended into the sky and from the sight of his disciples. Many examples of why people placed their faith and trust in Christ can be found throughout the New Testament. When Jesus said he was going to do something, he did it! Whether it was dying on the cross, giving his disciples the Holy Spirit to lead and guide his followers, or defeating death by rising from the dead after three days, he was and *always is* true to his promises.

Faith and trust, when it came to Christ and his ministry, were tools that he used in at least two significant ways. Either his actions planted the seeds of faith and trust in those around him that he was, in fact, the Son of God. Or Jesus reinforced the faith of those who believed they could be free from, for example, an affliction if they only trusted that he could make it so.

In the case of the former, a wonderful example is described in the eleventh chapter of John. In this account, John details the story of Lazarus's death that took place in the nearby village of Bethany about two miles from Jerusalem. When told that Lazarus is seriously ill, Jesus acknowledges his friend's condition, and promises to go visit him. To further build the faith and trust of his disciples he does just that, but does not leave immediately.

By the time the Lord keeps his commitment and reaches Bethany, a grief stricken Martha vents her frustration to him, and in John 11:21 Martha says, "…Lord, if you had been here, my brother would not have died." Yet, knowing that Jesus is the Son of God, she adds, "But even now I know whatever you ask from God, God will give you." John 11:22.

Reading between the lines, Martha expresses her grief and disappointment at having lost her brother because Jesus arrived too late. But she clearly demonstrates the strength of her faith and trust in Jesus when she adds, "…God will give you whatever you ask." She believes that Jesus can do anything. It's almost if, because of her deep faith, she's actually telling the Lord, "Yes, my brother would still be alive if you had come earlier, but my faith tells me you can bring him back from the dead if that is what you want to ask God for."

After Jesus had spoken with Martha for a short time, Martha went to Mary and told her that Jesus had arrived. Mary ran to meet him, her emotions overtaking her as she fell at his feet, spilling her heartache and tears. "Lord," she said, "if you had been here, my brother would not have died." John 11:32. Like Martha, she expresses her faith and trust in her savior by saying that because Christ is the Messiah, he could have stopped death from taking the brother she loved so deeply.

In the same chapter of John, verses 41–43, it is clear that Jesus wants to plant and grow the faith of those witnesses standing about him; that his intention is for them to believe he is the savior they have longed for. The verses read… "Then Jesus lifted up his eyes and said, 'Father, I thank you that you have heard me. I knew that you always hear me, but I said this on account of the people standing around, that they may believe that you sent me.'" Of course, when Lazarus does come back to life, many place their faith and trust in Jesus as the Christ.

A unique example of a time when Jesus strengthened the faith of a person with a physical malady was when he healed a woman who had been bleeding for over a decade. As the scripture says in Matthew 9:20–22, "Just then a woman who had been subject to bleeding for twelve years came up behind him and touched the edge of his cloak. She said to herself, 'If I only touch his cloak, I will be healed.' Jesus turned and saw her. 'Take heart, daughter,' he said, 'your faith has healed you.' And the woman was healed in that moment."

If the person asking for healing did not indicate that he trusted Jesus to cure him, the Lord asked the individual(s) if he or she believed he could. This was the case with two blind men in the same chapter (verses 27–30). When they both replied, "Yes, Lord," their sight was restored.

One of the most profound stories of faith in the New Testament is told in Matthew 8:5–10, "And when Jesus entered Capernaum, a centurion came to him, imploring him, and saying, 'Lord, my servant is lying paralyzed at home, fearfully tormented.' Jesus said to him, 'I will come and heal him.' But the centurion said, 'Lord, I am not worthy for you to come under my roof, but just say the word, and my servant will be healed. For I also am a man under authority, with soldiers under me; and I say to this one, 'Go!' and he goes, and to another, 'Come!' and he comes, and to my slave, 'Do this!' and he does it.' Now when Jesus heard this, he marveled and said to those who were following, 'Truly I say to you, I have not found such great faith with anyone in Israel.'"

In the above story, not only did the centurion show great reverence for the Lord in that he felt his home was not worthy for Jesus to enter, but he had such great faith that he knew if Jesus proclaimed his servant healed it was as good as done. And of course, when he returned to his home he discovered his servant was healed at the same instant Jesus said it would be so.

Can you imagine what it would be like to have a faith that amazes God himself? This is exactly the kind of faith that God wants and expects from us. He wants us to amaze him with our belief in him. God is not looking for mealy-mouthed Christians, who ask without great expectations, but Christians who know Jesus the Christ as the Lord of all creation and the God who is capable of anything!

It is essential that someone have faith and trust in Jesus Christ as the Son of God, in order to claim Christ as their personal savior. This is unmistakably illustrated in the gospels. Whether Jesus instilled faith and trust in those around him by publicly proclaiming that that was his purpose before healing someone, or if he simply complimented someone on the strength of their faith and healed them because of it, one thing is certain: faith and trust are essential ingredients to belief in Christ as one's personal Savior. It is no wonder then that Jesus placed such great emphasis upon them when he healed anyone.

Of course, no look at the tools of faith and trust from a biblical perspective would be complete without examining what took place when the disciples were caught in a storm on the Sea of Galilee and suddenly saw Christ walking on the water. The scene is painted by Matthew in the fourteenth chapter of his gospel:

"During the fourth watch of the night Jesus went out to them, walking on the lake. When the disciples saw him walking on the lake, they were terrified. 'It's a ghost,' they said, and cried out in fear. But Jesus immediately said to them: 'Take courage! It is I. Don't be afraid.'" Matthew 14:25-27

"'Lord, if it's you,' Peter replied, 'tell me to come to you on the water.'" Matthew 14:28

"'Come,' he said. Then Peter got down out of the boat, walked on the water and came toward Jesus. But when he saw the wind, he was afraid and,

beginning to sink, cried out, 'Lord, save me!' Immediately Jesus reached out his hand and caught him. 'You of little faith,' he said, 'why did you doubt?'"
Matthew 14:29-31

Unlike the other disciples, Peter's faith is tested in the crucible of a literal, terrible storm on the water. With wind howling, an angry sea frothing round about a storm-tossed boat in the darkness, the disciples see what they think is a ghost. Everyone is terrified, but Peter speaks up and, true to form, impulsively steps on the water to meet his Master.

Dissimilar to the other miracles Jesus performed where the person(s) healed declared their faith and trust first or were asked by Jesus if they believed, Jesus here invites Peter to trust him under the worst possible, most frightening conditions. But like we do in our own lives, we get distracted by the storms of stress around us, take our eyes off the Lord and soon find ourselves faint of heart and a faith. From Peter's experience, it's easy to see where our focus needs to be so that our faith and trust remains strong.

There is one more unique characteristic about this event that makes it stand out from all the others in the New Testament; Peter himself becomes a barometer, a measuring stick of the strength of his faith in Christ the very instant he steps out on the water. When he climbs overboard, walks and fixes his trust in the Lord, he is above the churning sea. When he's distracted by the raging torrent, lightning and winds and fear begins to rule, and he sinks.

Finally, we would be remiss as authors if we didn't mention Hebrews chapter 11. It is known as "The Hall of Faith" and is suggested reading because it reviews those who were faithful across the length and breadth of the Old Testament.

As His Apprentices:

Mark 5:25–34 "And there was a woman who had had a discharge of blood for twelve years, and had suffered much under many physicians, and had spent all that she had, and was no better but rather grew worse. She had the reports about Jesus and came up behind him in the crowd and touched his garment. For she said, 'If I touch even his garments, I will be made well.' And immediately the flow of blood dried up, and she felt in her body that she was healed of her disease.

And Jesus, perceiving in himself that the power had gone out from him immediately turned about in the crowd and said, 'Who touched my garments?' And his disciples said to him, 'You see the crowd pressing around you, and yet you say, 'Who touched me?' And he looked around to see who had done it.

But the woman knowing what had happened to her, came in fear and trembling and fell down before him. And told him the whole truth. And he said to her, 'Daughter, your faith has made you well; go in peace, and be healed of your disease.'" (ESV)

Matthew 8:8–10 "… 'But just say the word and my servant will be healed.' '…I tell you the truth, I have not found anyone in Israel with such great faith.'"

Commentary:

"You've got to believe in something…" said the bumper sticker. "I believe I'll have another beer." As the saying goes, "There's a grain of truth behind every joke" and this one liner is no exception. Millions of Americans use and abuse drugs and alcohol in an attempt to fill a void that materialism cannot and to numb themselves to the stresses of modern life. And of course, millions of people that never touch the stuff suffer collateral damage from the abusers, many carrying the scars of emotional and physical abuse for the rest of their lives (something one of the authors saw firsthand while working as clinical social worker).

In a Christian nation that has fallen far from its roots, the majority of our citizens are searching for meaning; something capable of holding their fragile trust and placing their faith in. Illicit drugs and all manner of humanistic philosophies have not provided an answer with a rock solid foundation that gives humans a sense of purpose and destiny. Only one person can do that, and his name is Jesus Christ.

Examples of a Believer's Use of the Tool:

Almost 20 years ago, when my husband John decided he didn't want to be married anymore, he left me and our two daughters, then 9 and 6-years-old. So began a chapter of my journey during which God revealed his character to me in astonishing new ways. He taught me that *he* is all I need. And did so in many creative, personal loving moments of gently prying my tightly clenched hands loose from all the stuff I had trusted. Then, once I was emptied out, what he gave me was so delightfully unexpected and perfect.

My husband walked away from our house, deeded it over *for free*, and gave me full custody of the children. A Christian education for my girls, paid by the church—my employer at the time—proved to be an immeasurable blessing, as they grew up knowing a God's eye perspective of the world. He gave them hearts of contentment: they never complained about cost-cutting, foregoing pricey presents to make fun new traditions for birthdays and holidays, shopping clearance racks, sharing a hand-me-down vehicle. They excelled at softball—cheap for me, richly rewarding for them. They've said more than once, it's good they grew up "poor" (though not really—we never went hungry). From a young age, they learned what's real and what's not.

I was a housewife when the church took a chance and hired me on as receptionist. When we gradually realized I had a head for numbers (who'd a-thought?!) they moved me over to the accounting department, then sent me to the local community college and paid for classes. What I learned in the morning, I used that afternoon.

The Lord taught me tools for trusting him. "Give us this day our daily bread…" I didn't need to worry about paying for next year or even next week; I was cupped in his hands. And my attitude was of giving with the knowledge that we can't ever out-give God. That it's not just about money, it's also about offering our talents and our time (serving the Children's and Music ministries was fulfilling and beneficial) as well as our hearts (cooking for those under the weather or grieving), and most importantly our prayers; bearing fellow sojourners to the Throne in intercessory prayer. The Christ of the loaves and fishes is still multiplying our contributions.

Now, all these years later, I look back at that time as wonderful progress toward the realization that the things we have that we can see are bestowed by God to serve his purposes in our lives, and as a means to an end—to conform us to Christ's image. A tremendous compliment I once received from a pastor will always stay with me: "You hold things very loosely," he observed. Words of encouragement from God's heart to mine.

When I look around at others who have more or less than I have, I'm assured that God's plan for me—for all of us—is perfect. And as I move forward to whatever amazing-ness is next, I enjoy clothes shopping at Savers and Goodwill—there is some very cool stuff there. I love whisking my creative juices by finding household furnishings and accessories at garage sales. I like buzzing around in my little second-hand economy car, and I buy supplies at the dollar store that I used to pay much more for elsewhere. There is joyful satisfaction in finding resourceful ways of running a home on a smaller income.

And I'm thunderstruck with awe and worship for all the *intangible* blessings and lessons he's poured into my world. My cup runneth over. It's all good because God is more than I can imagine, and because he initiated a Covenant.

If there is anything that tests a father's faith in God and shakes the very foundation of his trust in a loving, benevolent Creator, it's watching his child suffer and being powerless to do a single thing about it. Well, except pray. But this is where my wife Kris, my family and I found ourselves over a 10-day period several years ago.

Our daughter Mackenzie was born with hydrocephalus. This is usually a congenital condition in which an abnormal accumulation of fluid in the cerebral ventricles causes an enlargement of the skull and compression of the brain, destroying much of the neural tissue. We were told that she would require a shunt. When she was in junior high school her shunt failed.

Before I get any further, I have to communicate how proud I am of how our daughter handled the entire situation. She never once expressed self pity, never complained, never quit fighting and never said "Why me?" She faced every challenge and overcame it.

In 2002, our then 17-year-old daughter had been having headaches on and off for about two weeks and they were particularly bad when she was lying down. We couldn't get in to see our doctor until the following week, but were advised by our physician to go to the emergency room if the headaches got worse.

The headaches did worsen and we took Mackenzie to the hospital. On the way she started vomiting and was in severe pain so we took her directly to the emergency room. Kris and I stayed at her bedside as they examined, x-rayed and treated her for the pain. It took until 3:00 or 4:00 AM until they got us a diagnosis. The x-rays revealed that the tube in her chest had broken and was not allowing her shunt to drain properly. Our physician was called and our daughter was transported by ambulance to Phoenix Children's Hospital.

Kris and I had always known that a shunt failure was a possibility and that a routine procedure would correct it. Surgery was scheduled for that afternoon. After the operation the doctor told us our daughter was fine, that he'd replaced the old shunt, and that some of it was left in but wouldn't cause any problems. As a result of the surgery she was completely free of the headaches. Needless to say, we were relieved and thankful to have the worst behind us.

I called the hospital the next day to check on Mackenzie and discovered her headaches had returned and that she had been transferred to ICU during the night for treatment. I immediately went to the hospital and one of the doctors told me the reason for the pain and that he would have to operate to relieve it. Our hearts sank at the news but we both knew if we continued to put our faith in God everything would be okay no matter what happened.

During the surgery my wife and I sat in the waiting room as hours crawled slowly by without a word. I can't even begin to describe how beside ourselves we were with worry (believe me, faith grows by leaps in bounds in moments like these!). I just tried as hard as I could not to show it so that Kris wouldn't be as upset as I was. Finally, the surgeon met us along with a female social worker. The look on their faces wasn't good. We were told that Mackenzie had had seizures while in surgery, that she was still not awake and not responding to verbal commands. Because of that he said they were keeping her on a respirator.

We rushed to our daughter's room and found her lying in bed with hoses, tubes, wires and monitors everywhere. Doctors and nurses were caught up in a flurry of activity around our girl. The fear I felt for her was something I can't put into words.

When the sun came up there was still no change. We kept talking to our child as if she could hear us. Kris and I just wanted her to squeeze our fingers or wiggle her toes...nothing. We never left her side except when one of us needed to go off to a quiet place to cry and pray for our daughter's recovery. Never in our lives had we poured our hearts out to our Heavenly Father like those days in the hospital; never had our faith grown so strong. God was working in our lives, strengthening us with each situation we faced.

Early that afternoon Mackenzie began to throw up. It was horrible. Her body went into convulsions and I could see the pain in her face. I had to leave the room. When the nurses came out they told us our girl was fine and that they had taken the respirator out.

Not long after that ordeal we received more bad news. Our doctor told us that x-rays now showed that fluid was accumulating in Mackenzie's lungs and it was decided to put her back on the respirator. The challenge now was to clear them and was accomplished by hourly visits from the physical therapist that pounded her on her back, put a respirator tube into her lungs, and sucked the fluid out. Each time it threw Mackenzie into convulsions and was horrible to watch. I wished I could take my daughter's place and at the same time wondered how God could possibly let his son die on the cross.

As a result of the trauma of having to do this so often, Mackenzie began to thrash around. Her legs were tied down but she continued to fight. The only solution was to give her a drug that paralyzed her. But there was a positive side; the doctor said this movement was a good sign.

By this time we had contacted family and friends. Word spread fast and we were placed on many prayer lists. People were praying for us that we hardly knew. Many of our friends wanted to come to the hospital to be with, support and pray with us but I wasn't ready for visitors.

Early on a subsequent morning our doctor showed us x-rays of our daughter's lungs. They were significantly better. Later the same morning came an answer to prayer! I will never forget that feeling when I asked Mackenzie to squeeze my finger and I felt her precious little hand squeeze mine ever so slightly. It was as if I felt the Holy Spirit of God come through her body and into my heart. My eyes filled with tears of joy—she was coming back.

Over the next several hours Mackenzie was wiggling her toes and squeezing our fingers on command. Her lungs continued to clear and later that afternoon a nurse took the respirator out. Our girl was breathing on her own. By that evening she was speaking softly and taking ice chips and small pieces of a Popsicle.

By morning the next day Mackenzie was speaking clearly and had no complaints of a headache, but a new challenge developed: hallucinations. She kept seeing babies and small children in and around her bed. At first it seemed innocent and almost funny except that it went on all day and into the evening.

Further, the hallucinations made our daughter believe that she had forgotten about a child she was caring for or thought that a baby at the foot of her bed had fallen to the floor. When this happened she would panic and try to get out of bed. No matter what we said we could not convince her otherwise. I recall watching the news of a major forest fire near our cabin in Northern Arizona and thinking how insignificant that event was even if our cabin burned down. All we cared about was our daughter.

But God was definitely working in our lives giving us the strength and faith we needed to get from day to day. Kris left the room and went out to visit with friends and they prayed together for our daughter. Mackenzie gained her strength back slowly and was able to take short walks.

I'll leave out many of the details, but our daughter went through a night of horrific hallucinations filled with terror and fear beyond belief. It started an hour or so after she took a sleeping pill. She became very disoriented and didn't know where she was, except she knew she had to get both of us out of there no matter what it took. I was neither able to distract her nor settle her down. She was constantly trying to get out of bed and tearing the IVs out of her arms every few minutes.

The I.V. needed to be replaced at one point and Mackenzie would not let that happen. It took a team of nurses and eventually the resident doctor to restrain her; she was kicking and fighting with all of her might. All during that time she kept trying to whisper to me that we needed to leave the room because the medical staff was trying to kill us.

What followed next was as if the devil himself loomed over us. Different and ever-frightening hallucinations waged war in my daughter's mind for the rest of the evening and far into the early morning. I saw such terror in her eyes at one point that I had to turn my head away. I was deathly afraid of what she saw when she looked at me; my face appearing like Satan, confirming her worst fear that "...they'd (the staff) killed me." On top of that, I simply could not bear to look at the tenderhearted daughter I loved since the moment I first saw her.

But I couldn't, didn't lose my faith inside the worst of it, even though there were moments when I felt pushed beyond my limits. Somehow God gave my wife and I, our family the strength we needed when we needed it. If that wasn't true we would not have survived the experience.

The hallucinations and disorientation were gone the next morning and nobody was certain why. Maybe the pill she was given earlier on was working, maybe because many other medications were removed, or maybe her body and mind simply gained strength back. They kept her in ICU for the next two days and she was taking regular walks and going downstairs to eat with us. It was a thrill to see her grow stronger each day.

Eventually she was moved out of ICU into a regular room. Friends came by with gifts and flowers to wish her well. Late that morning our doctor came to check on Mackenzie. Her lungs were clear, all vital signs were good, and she continued to gain strength. All thumbs were up and our doctor suggested we take our daughter home. Hallelujah! Praise God! We had our precious girl back!

It had been 10 days that seemed like an eternity. Kris and I never spoke of it, but at one point we both weren't sure if our daughter was ever going to squeeze our fingers or wiggle her toes. It was in God's hands and it was through faith in him that we found the strength and trust to outlast the most difficult circumstances we have ever faced.

3. The Tool of OBEDIENCE

Tool Verses:

John 14:23 "If anyone loves me, he will obey my teaching. My Father will love him, and we will come to him and make our home with him. He who does not love me will not obey my teaching. These words you hear are not my own; they belong to the Father who sent me."

1 Peter 1:14-15 "As obedient children, do not conform to the evil desires you had when you lived in ignorance. But just as he who called you is holy, so be holy in all you do…"

2 John 1:6 "And this is love: that we walk in obedience to his commands. As you have heard from the beginning, his command is that you walk in love."

The Master Carpenter's Use of the Tool:

Many of the spiritual tools that lie ahead find their meaning and context with what Christ went through during his crucifixion, and obedience is no exception. As he hung on the cross he suffered horrendous physical and emotional pain and unimaginable agony. As if that wasn't enough for any man to bear, he became sin and gave his life for each one of us. Yet he remained steadfast in his obedience to the Father.

Scripture clearly points out in Philippians 2:6 that Jesus was, "Obedient to death—even death on the cross!" In the most basic terms, he did what the Father requested of him in every way, living a perfect life and turning it into an unblemished sacrifice.

In short, obedience is as important as love is to our Father and the 120+ verses referencing obedience in the New Testament are proof of this fact.

As His Apprentices:

John 14:21 "Whoever has my commands and obeys them, he is the one who loves me. He who loves me will be loved by my Father, and I too will love him and show myself to him."

John 14:23 "If anyone loves me, he will obey my teaching. My Father will love him, and we will come to him and make our home with him."

Commentary:

Nearly every day a miracle happens on the roadways of a major city in America. Across the country, citizens pull out of their driveways and, for the most part, obey the traffic laws and make it safely to their destinations.

I live in metropolitan area of some three million people, and I am often astounded when, at the height of the rush hour, when it seems that most of the populace is clogging up the asphalt, that the following traffic report often comes across the radio: "There are no accidents to report at this time..." Apparently, most Americans make the choice to be obedient on the streets and highways. Their motivation? Personal safety, and, of course, lower insurance rates.

Like motorists when it comes to following the rules of the road, as Christians we make the decision to accept Christ as Savior out of obedience. This is the first tool that God puts in our hands because without it, we could not find salvation and a personal relationship with Jesus Christ.

Further, after doing so we are to pick up our cross (defined earlier as difficult life circumstances). And crucify ourselves to our own desires and wills (Romans 6:6), just as Christ chose to pick up his literal cross and allowed himself to be crucified.

In fundamental terms, if you love the Lord, you will keep his commands. You will be obedient to him and follow after him without question. When I say without question, I mean without doubt. You may question why, but not with an attitude of disrespect like a disobedient child. Instead you follow; are obedient in faith knowing he has your best interests in mind.

When we pull on to the streets in our town or city, we choose to be obedient to the rules of the road. When we are faced with our cross, we choose to follow the will of God and walk in obedience to him. That, in the proverbial nutshell, is the Tool of Obedience.

Examples of a Believer's Use of the Tool:

My husband Dan and I had been married for 12 years and I knew full well that he had an ongoing problem with pornography. When I first discovered it, it made me sick and I wanted to run…I wanted to leave this man and never come back. I kept wondering how the fine Christian person I married could get so tangled up in something so evil and despicable.

In May of 2005 the Lord miraculously revealed it to me. I remember it so vividly. I held Dan, told him I knew about the pornography, and gave him permission to tell me all about it. I felt I needed to be obedient and stay by his side even though at that moment I felt like walking out the door. The story started at that moment, but I soon discovered my husband was keeping another secret from me.

First he confessed to having $30,000 of debt that I had been kept unaware of. And finally, he admitted that he had been meeting women over the Internet and had committed adultery with four of them over the last few years. I felt the Holy Spirit telling me not to leave. I felt God's message was clear: I had to be obedient and stay with my husband despite the fact that I knew I had grounds for divorce.

The pornography and the debt came as a shock, but I felt it was survivable. However, the adultery seemed too much to bear. The emotional pain was intense. A dear Christian friend gave me some advice but mainly just let me cry. I was determined to be obedient as my Lord desired and keep the marriage together, but was physically sick every time I was in my husband's presence. I was afraid I would have to seek medical help.

One day when I was driving to the store I felt a refreshing feeling come over me. I felt lifted up, strengthened and knew I was being restored. After that my illness was virtually gone.

It took several months for my husband's heart to soften. These were very difficult months when leaving would have been far easier than staying. But these were days that I can only describe as being "held by Jesus." Often I would read and pray through the Scripture four or five times a day. I was given a hope and joy only Christ can give and I learned lessons I will always be grateful for. Among them, how important it is to remain obedient to what God is calling you to do in the midst of a personal crisis.

Dan finally made the decision to stay in his faith and our marriage. It was the beginning of a road of great, great change for him. There have been bumps, but I can say that our marriage is better now than I ever imagined it ever could be, even as a newlywed. And Dan's faith and transformation is a constant spiritual encouragement to me. I never thought that obedience could so profoundly change us as a couple and give us a marriage we could have only dreamed of when we took our vows. God is so good!

I was born and raised on a farm in Wisconsin. Ever since I can remember, my parents took my sister, brother, and I to worship in a little one-room country church. The earliest advice I can remember my dad giving me was, "*The least* we can do for God is to worship on Sunday." This was in obedience to the commandment: "Remember the Sabbath day by keeping it holy."

That bit of advice has remained with me throughout my life. I was obedient to it when I went off to the University of Wisconsin. While other fellow students would sleep or stay in each Sunday, I would make my way to church to worship God.

After two years at the University of Wisconsin, I decided to join the Air Force since the Korean Conflict was on and the draft was threatening. Dad's advice still stuck with me and I continued to go to chapel services every Sunday.

I eventually ended up at Neubiberg Air Base outside of Munich, Germany. One Sunday, an evangelical chaplain visited our base, gave the morning sermon, and announced he would be preaching again that evening. I was so impressed that I returned that night. At that service he said that if anyone needed prayer to raise their hands (I thought I always needed prayer so I raised my hand).

At the conclusion of the service he invited all who raised their hands to meet with him in a side room of the chapel. After some discussion, he asked us to follow him in a prayer of commitment and to ask Jesus to come into our lives. Although I was a nominal Christian, I did not fully understand the implication of that prayer.

Some time later, the Air Force wing stationed at Neubiberg Air Base made the move to a new air base at Landstuhl, Germany. The chaplain of the base had been the visiting chaplain at Neubiberg and I became involved in a Bible study on the base. One weekend the chaplain arranged for a spiritual retreat. Twelve of us airman signed up to attend. It was on that retreat that I had my spiritual conversion or came to Christ and realized what the meaning of committing one's life to Jesus Christ really meant.

Early one morning the chaplain had us read from Psalm 139: "Search me, O God, and know my heart; test me, and know my anxious thoughts. See if there is any offensive way in me, and lead me in the way everlasting." Each of us went off by ourselves to meditate on that verse. As I sat alone I decided I would be obedient and do what it said; I allowed God to search my heart.

He revealed to me what a hypocrite I had been-pretending to be a good Christian before the chaplain and the other men in the Bible study group on Sunday, but drinking and carousing with other guys during the week. God showed me that I could not have it both ways. It had to be one or the other. If I was going to follow Christ, it had to be all the way and all of me.

Sometime later, the chaplain asked me what I was going to do after being discharged from the Air Force. He suggested that I consider the ordained ministry. I said, "No way!" I had excuses: I had a speech impediment, I didn't like being and speaking in front of people, I wasn't intelligent enough to make it through seminary and I couldn't afford it financially (it would take two more years of college and three years of seminary). They were all legitimate reasons—or so I thought.

The chaplain never pressured me about going into the ministry. However, one day he asked, "Are you willing to do anything God asks you to do?"

"Of course," I said.

"Then what about the ministry?" he asked.

I was trapped. As I listened to God's voice, it became evident that was what he was telling me to do. Once again, I had to be obedient and faithful to God's calling.

I've been retired from the ministry for nearly a decade after serving 35 years as a pastor. And in my retirement have served in two churches in part time positions and one year as an interim pastor in a third church.

Being obedient to God's call and purpose in life is the only way to live a life that is abundant and full. The hymn writer, James H. Sammis put it this way: "Trust and obey, for there's no other way. To be happy in Jesus, but to trust and obey."

4. The Tool of INTERCESSION

Tool Verses:

Matthew 6:5 "And when you pray, do not be like the hypocrites, for they love to pray standing in the synagogues and on the street corners to be seen by men. I tell you the truth, they have received their reward in full."

Matthew 6:6 "But when you pray, go into your room, close the door and pray to your Father, who is unseen. Then your Father, who sees what is done in secret, will reward you."

Matthew 6:9 "This, then, is how you should pray: 'Our Father in heaven, hallowed be your name, your kingdom come, your will be done on earth as it is in heaven.'"

Luke 6:27–28 "But I tell you who hear me: Love your enemies, do good to those who hate you, bless those who curse you, pray for those who mistreat you."

The Master Carpenter's Use of the Tool:

Jesus showed us how to pray after one of the disciples asked him to demonstrate it by reciting what we now know as the "The Lord's Prayer" (Matthew 6:9-13). Not only did Jesus teach his disciples how to intercede for others. He, on many occasions, told the disciples that he needed time alone to pray. The Master Carpenter made it a priority to pray often, and we, as his apprentices walking stride for stride with him, need to do the same.

What is clear in the gospels is that prayer served a few different purposes for Jesus. The first was to gain peace and strength, for instance when he was in the garden of Gethsemane or facing other challenges. Secondly to provide forgiveness for each one present during the crucifixion as well as those millions of believers to come in the two millennia that have followed.

Furthermore, in every instance that Jesus healed anyone of a disease or infirmity, he prayed to the Father that the person would be healed. The only exception was the woman who was healed by touching his garment in Mark Chapter 5. And in the case of Lazarus, as noted earlier, he prayed aloud that the act of raising his friend from the dead would glorify God (John 11:40) and benefit the people who were there with him, that they might believe that he (Jesus) was sent by the God the Father. (John 11:42)

Finally, we've talked about the importance of Jesus' relationship with God the Father and noted that he himself said, "I and the Father are one." And that his profession of carpentry was a constant reminder of what was to come and led him to pray constantly for the strength to walk the road he knew he must follow.

As His Apprentices:

1 Thessalonians 5:16–18 "Be joyful always; pray continually; give thanks in all circumstances, for this is God's will for you in Christ Jesus."

Ephesians 6:18 "And pray in the Spirit on all occasions with all kinds of prayers and requests. With this in mind, be alert and always keep on praying for all the saints."

Commentary:

As Christians, nearly every one of us knows someone whose life was drastically changed by prayer. Perhaps the individual was healed from a disease, drug addiction, or some other destructive habit. Or perhaps you know of someone who received an unexpected monetary gift that was just the right amount to pay an over due bill.

Most Christians believe that prayer is an effective tool for physical and psychological healing and whether or not science agrees is a moot point. As believers we've seen countless prayers answered and know that a loving God is at the center of it, and it is not mere coincidence. As the saying in Christian circles goes, "God always answers prayer."

We also know that know that his answer or response to our prayers isn't always what we are hoping for. But, whether or not God answers our prayer in the manner in which we desire is not the point here. We are admonished by the apostle Paul on more than one occasion to "pray without ceasing" and to be "in prayer and supplication" making our requests known to him. Our point is that we are commanded to pray and it is through prayer that our communion with God is blessed and he is pleased.

Examples of a Believer's Use of the Tool:

It was in 1986 when my wife Rhonda and I came to know Jesus Christ as our personal Lord and Savior. And like many new believers, we were anxious and excited to share our newfound faith in Christ with those we loved, especially our parents. I first met Earl when I started dating his daughter (now my wife) at the age of 17. The meeting couldn't have gone better. The fact that I had short hair and wore a cowboy hat and boots definitely worked in my favor.

Earl was born in Phoenix, Arizona in the winter of 1930. His parents had come to Arizona during the Great Depression along with many others from Oklahoma in order to start a new life. And Phoenix, though it would be hard to tell now, was a quaint, small-time country town. It was a place where being a cowboy or at least looking like one was typical, and Earl was no exception to the norm.

It was a rare occasion to see him without his boots on. And the only time he wasn't wearing a cowboy hat was when he was inside. He was a rugged man, a U.S. Steelworker for over 30 years, a Korean War veteran, and a proud American.

Rhonda and I began dating during our senior year in high school though we went to different schools. We continued dating throughout our four years at Arizona State University until we were married in February of 1985. After getting married we immediately moved to San Diego, California where I took a job in sales working for a large multi-national corporation.

It was in San Diego where we got involved in the Amway® business. Like many others, we got involved with the anticipation of making millions before the age of 30. We never did, but it was at an Amway® meeting in Southern California where we both responded to the call of Christ during a Sunday morning worship service. Well, if it wasn't enough that we had gotten into Amway®, now we had become "born again" Christians. Eventually Rhonda and I became inactive in Amway®, but as time went on we became more active in our church in California, and even more so when we moved back to Phoenix.

Holidays for Rhonda and I were often spent traveling from my mom's house to her parent's home, often enjoying two holiday suppers every Thanksgiving and Christmas. It was at these family gatherings that I was often called upon to pray before dinner. When at my in-laws the invitation to do so often came from Earl, but usually in the form of joke. I recall on more than one occasion when Earl would quip, "We need to wait for Larry to talk to his plate before we can eat."

Though I knew that Earl never meant anything by his remarks, they often saddened me. Not because I felt that his comments were directly at me personally, but because my desire was for him to see the truth of "Who" I was praying to; the God of the universe who loved him more than he could possibly imagine. As time passed I continued to pray at these family meals. But more importantly, I prayed regularly that Earl would come to know God through his son Jesus Christ.

After a few years, Rhonda and I became the parents of three sons. But just shortly after the birth of our third son, Rhonda's mom Charlotte, who we all loved dearly, passed away after a long bout with lung cancer. With the loss of Charlotte, Earl was now not only lost spiritually, but emotionally as well. To this day I feel that Earl missed Charlotte more than any of us knew.

Earl soon began to spend even more time with Rhonda, the boys and I and we enjoyed having him around. Dinner at our house was always a welcome invitation to "Papa" and he often came over to savor his daughter's home cooking. As we sat around the dining room table Papa would often talk about the "old days." We all enjoyed listening to him tell stories about how he sold cantaloupes from his wagon as a kid and got into fights as a teenager. The boys especially liked hearing about Papa's hot rod cars and the war. One funny, but true story Papa told us was about how his mother cried and cried when his brother Ralph was drafted during WWII. But when Earl left to fight in Korea his mom had said, "That's okay, Earl likes to fight." And if his stories were any indication, it was very true!

On occasion, when the timing seemed right, I would share the gospel with Earl. But his response was always the same. He would make remarks like, "If I go to church the roof will cave in." Or, "Well, at least when I go to hell, I'll have seniority." I guess he figured that since he lived in Phoenix his entire life, where in mid July it could be "hotter than hell," as he said it, he was sure to have a high rank there. As had always been the case, I was dismayed by his remarks. But I never stopped praying to the Father, "God, let him see you. Draw him to yourself Lord."

I'll admit I had little faith that God would draw Earl to Himself. The man seemed so hard, so determined not to give in. But Jesus calls us to have the faith of a child. And though Jesus never said it per se, I think he wants us to be as open and outspoken as children often are. For example, in the evenings as we would sit down for dinner with Papa at the head of the table, I'd often call on one of my sons to offer thanks. As they took turns saying grace on respective nights, in their childlike boldness each would say, "God, please help Papa to become a Christian." My sons were never concerned that Papa was sitting right there. I guess they figured that he might as well know they were praying for him. Wow, what a concept! Every night, when I put my boys to bed we prayed, "Dear God, please help Papa to become a Christian."

In early June of 2005 Earl, who was more a dad to me than a father-in-law, was hospitalized with a blood clot in each of his lungs and four in one of his legs. When he was first admitted to the hospital the doctors were cautiously optimistic. However, deep inside I feared that he would die. After all, the pulmonary specialist said that he had never seen anyone still alive with a blood clot as large as Earl had in his left lung.

I am ashamed to admit that as I prayed for Earl's health and salvation, I was more concerned with having to tell my sons that they weren't going to see their grandfather in heaven if Earl died without Christ as personal Savior. How would I explain that in God's sovereign plan, Papa never accepted Christ? I knew if this happened that their tender hearts would be burdened with more than the grief of his loss.

While in the hospital, I would often visit Earl in the evenings and Rhonda would be with him during the day. One night as we sat and watched TV and talked on and off, he would drift off to sleep as would I. About 10:30 PM I said, "Well, I better get home, dad." He agreed and I said a brief prayer to comfort him. Before I left I reminded him, "Remember dad, there are a lot of people praying for you. And the doctors said you'll be going home in a few days. Don't lose hope dad. I love you."

As I think back on that moment now, I can almost picture our Father in heaven leaning over to Jesus and the Holy Spirit and saying, "Wait'll Larry sees this!" For as I turned to leave Earl stopped me.

"Larry?" he said.

"Yeah dad," I responded.

"Larry, how can I have the Lord in my life?"

For a moment I was speechless. I truly *could not* believe my ears. Then I said, "If that's how you truly feel in your heart dad, he's already there."

Well, needless to say, I helped Earl pray as he confessed his sin and accepted Jesus Christ as his personal Lord and Savior. We talked afterward for about an hour and prayed together again. I went home. I was barely out of the parking lot when I called Rhonda to give her the great news.

Earl died two weeks later on July 3rd. I delivered the eulogy at his funeral and sang, "If You Could See Me Now." I think of Earl often and I miss him dearly, but God answered my prayers and those of our family. I look forward to the day when I will see him again in heaven.

In the early morning on a Sunday in March 1996 I was pulled abruptly from a deep slumber by the sound of my telephone ringing. It was my mom. She was having difficulty breathing and asked me to come to her nearby home and drive her to the hospital. I quickly jumped into a pair of blue jeans, threw on a shirt and shoes, and must have set new land speed record covering the mile between my house and hers. As I did I tried not to think the worst. But as it turned out, that didn't matter much.

After coming to a screeching halt in the driveway I ran into the house in a panic. I found her on the floor barely breathing. I hurriedly got her into my car, jumped in and took off. I sped down a major thoroughfare in Phoenix doing a blinding 90 mph. I glanced over at my mom as the desert landscape flew past in blur. She was slumped over in the seat. She had stopped breathing. I instinctively knew she would die before I reached the hospital. Fear had me in a death grip of its own.

I slammed the accelerator to the floorboard. The needle jumped to 100 mph. I put a stranglehold on the steering wheel. The image of fire station I'd passed for years flashed across my mind. I pulled into the driveway and came to another screeching stop. I leaped from my car and sprinted to the door. It was locked!

I frantically pounded on the door. No answer! "Wake up! Wake up! My mom is dying!" I screamed. My pounding and screaming awoke the entire station house and several firemen poured out as if I'd opened some giant valve. I directed them to my car. Two firemen yanked my mom from the front passenger seat like she was a rag doll. Others sprinted to get emergency medical equipment from the fire truck and ambulance in a display of teamwork that that would have left any NASCAR pit crew speechless.

Everything seemed to go into hyper slow motion...I remember one fireman barking out orders. Another yelled, "Full code, no vitals!" They laid my mom down gently on the cold cement of the driveway and frantically performed CPR. As several firemen worked to bring my mom back to life another one calmly escorted me from the scene to the back of the station. I could hear the concern in the firemen's voices as the door closed behind us and we walked through the garage.

Was I too late? Was my mother going to die on the cold, concrete driveway of a big city fire station?   It was surreal.

I trembled with fear and worry. I held my head in my hands and paced back and forth. Then suddenly my thoughts turned to Philippians 2:25–28. This is where Paul tells about how his dear friend Epaphroditus was ill to the point of death. Paul states that God had mercy on his friend, but also on Paul. He said that God spared him (Paul) "sorrow upon sorrow" in healing his beloved brother in Christ.

As I fell to my knees, tears streamed down my face. I cried out to the Lord, "God please don't take my mom, I'm not ready to lose her. *Please* God don't take her now!" My mom was not a Christian. To lose her now would be to lose her *forever*.

I can't remember for the life of me how I got there, but my next memory was being in the front passenger seat of the ambulance with lights flashing and sirens blaring speeding down the road to the hospital. In the back of the ambulance the firefighters were working feverishly to revive my mother. I was only able to get a quick glance at her as the firemen wheeled her stretcher swiftly toward the Emergency Room doors where the doctors and ER staff emerged and took over. She looked lifeless, her lips blue from lack of oxygen.

As I waited in the hospital minutes turned into hours. It would be an eternity before I would see her again.

I called my wife and told her what was happening. I don't really remember much after that, except one of my pastors was suddenly there next to me. Finally a doctor came with the news: despite the fact that the firemen had restarted my mother's heart, she had suffered complete respiratory failure, going 11 minutes without oxygen. Miraculously, she was alive. But the physicians were very guarded and gave little hope. Chances were that she would die soon. They suggested that I call family members and let them know they needed to come quickly if they wanted to say their final goodbyes.

I immediately began calling my brother and five sisters. With two sisters in Iowa and one in New Hampshire I didn't know if there would be enough time. But mom held on long enough for my sisters to get to Phoenix. In fact, she lay in coma for 11 days. Testing (EEGs) showed little brain activity.

Much time was spent in prayer during those 11 days; prayers said in silence by each family member as well as many prayers led by pastors and friends who were with us at the hospital and at our home. On day 12, my mom opened her eyes, but she was unable to speak or even move. But she was awake!

Eventually she was moved to a facility for those who required special medical attention. This was in part because she had to be on a ventilator in order to breathe, but that also kept her from eating. For several months she had to receive nourishment through a feeding tube that went directly into her stomach. Later she was transferred to another facility to help wean her off of the ventilator. This took almost a year, but eventually she was able to breathe without help. Even so, she was still unable to speak and required around the clock care and extensive physical therapy.

About a year after I'd raced to her house, we moved my mom to a long-term care facility in North Phoenix called Christian Care. They fed, bathed and took tremendous care of my mother for the entire time she was there. There was a young lady who went to my church that worked at the facility that visited mom daily, reading her the never-ending supply of letters from oldest sister. The social director there, Ellen, took a special interest in my mother, reading scripture to and praying with her as well. I visited her regularly and did the same.

My mother had been at that same facility for about four years when I received the most bizarre and shocking phone call from Ellen. Remember, Ellen had been visiting my mother regularly for years by this time. The phone call went something like this:

"Hi Larry, Ellen calling," she said, sounding very excited, which had me thoroughly confused. "Don't worry, everything is okay." she quickly added.

"Hi Ellen", I said.

"Larry, I met your mom today!"

Even more baffled, I said, "What do you mean you 'met my mom,' Ellen?! She's been living there for four years!"

"I know Larry. But I met your *mom* today," she said.

"What are you talking about, Ellen?" I said incredulously. She went on to explain that she and a nurse had visited my mom's room shortly after lunch. She was sitting up in bed when Ellen and the nurse walked in. From the day she rode in the ambulance until I received that phone call, all she was capable of doing was lying down; sitting up required special help from another person and special medical equipment for support. However, her communication had improved somewhat, but even those who saw her daily could barely understand her when she attempted to speak.

As Ellen and the nurse stood spellbound next to her bed, my mom turned to them and said, "I want to know Jesus Christ as my Savior." The two of them didn't know whether to faint, scream, jump up and down or pinch themselves. As soon as they got over the initial shock, Ellen and the nurse spent the next 20 minutes talking with my mom and leading her to Christ. She said it was as if there was nothing wrong with her at all. She was as lucid as could be.

After awhile, my mom told Ellen she was tired and wanted to rest. She lay quietly down and went to sleep. A short time later, Ellen returned to mom's bedside to find her back in her usual condition, lying in bed and unable to communicate or do anything for herself. My mother continued to live at that care center for about 8 years until she went home to be with God in December of 2004.

Sometimes when I think back on the horrific day in March 1996 I ask myself, "Why didn't I call 911?" And I like to think if I had it to over again I would have done just that. Perhaps if the firemen could have gotten to my mom just a bit sooner, the brain damage would have been prevented, and the entire horrible ordeal, along with her lengthy stay at Christian Care would have been avoided. It's said that hindsight is always 20/20. Perhaps it is, but that doesn't mean that hindsight is always right.

When I think of the prayer I cried out on my knees behind the fire station that day, I have to praise God. I praise him not for just allowing me to have my mom with me for another eight years here on earth, but for drawing her to Himself in such a wondrous and miraculous way that only he could do. Praise and glory to our God, forever and ever, amen! Praise God I will see her again one day!

5. The Tool of FORGIVENESS

Tool Verses:

Colossians 2:13–14 "He forgave all our sins. He canceled the debt, which listed all the rules we failed to follow. He took away that record with its rules and nailed it to the cross (paraphrase by Max Lucado)."

Psalm 103:2–5 "Praise the Lord, O my soul, and forget not all his benefits who forgives all your sins and heals all your diseases, who redeems your life from the pit and crowns you with love and compassion, who satisfies your desires with good things so that your youth is renewed like the eagle's."

Luke 23:34 "Jesus said, 'Father, forgive them, for they do not know what they are doing.'"

The Master Carpenter's Use of the Tool:

We must again return to Calvary for the Lord's use of the Tool of Forgiveness. The scenes of Christ reaching Golgotha with the cross have already been examined. After the Lord carried the cross to the top of the hill, he was nailed to it and the cross-dropped into a hole in the ground to keep it upright. It was at this precise moment that our Lord's suffering was magnified.

With the gravity of the very world he created pulling down on his body, our Savior was forced to use his pierced feet to support his weight. The searing pain from doing merely that must have been hard enough to handle as a human, but when he tried to relieve that agony with his arms, it pulled on the spikes that had already pierced holes in his hands. And that is to say nothing of the relentless pain resulting from the lashing, physical and emotional abuse as well as the crown of thorns he allowed others to place on his head.

Somehow, in some way, the Lord rose above it and found the strength to utter the words so strikingly captured in the gospel of Luke. In verse 23:34 Jesus said, "Father, forgive them, for they do not know what they are doing." This is another moment when the Son of God used a spiritual tool as only the Master Carpenter could, and after having allowed the literal tools of the cross to take such a huge toll on his body and spirit. No one before or since has used both in the same way and with the salvation of mankind hanging in the balance along with the Savior himself.

As His Apprentices:

Luke 6:37 "Do not judge, and you will not be judged. Do not condemn, and you will not be condemned. Forgive, and you will be forgiven."

Colossians 3:13 "Bear with each other and forgive whatever grievances you may have against one another. Forgive as the Lord forgave you."

Matthew 18:21–22 "Then Peter came to Jesus and asked, 'Lord, how many times shall I forgive my brother when he sins against me? Up to seven times?' Jesus answered, 'I tell you, not seven times, but seventy times seven.'"

Commentary:

Is there a harder question for a human being to ask than, "Will you forgive me?" Yet, there's probably no other query in the English language that has the power to restore a relationship, no matter the depth of the hurt caused by the transgression.

Some would argue that asking forgiveness of someone you've wronged is harder than granting forgiveness. While that may be open for debate, there are few that would argue the unfathomable depth of Christ's love for us that allowed him to forgive those responsible for his treatment just prior to and for his death upon the cross.

Imagine the greatest emotional hurt your have ever known in your lifetime. Now add to that the agony Christ endured on the cross as a result of the crucifixion. Place that on top of the fact that you were railroaded through a justice system that, despite your total innocence, found you guilty by those in your own community. Many of these people probably even knew you since your childhood. By doing so, you have experienced a mere inkling of what Christ suffered on the cross.

Somehow, even in his humanness he found the strength, the human capacity to forgive those who put him on a cross at the top of that hill, forgive the disciples who denied him, forgive the sins of a thief on the cross next to him, AND pay for our sins at the same time. Forgiveness on top of forgiveness on top of forgiveness was still another way that Jesus stacked the deck in our favor to demonstrate the awesome love he has for each one of us.

Examples of a Believer's Use of the Tool:

My father died in 1965. He was killed at the age of 37 while protecting a woman from an abusive husband. I was only 3-years-old at the time, and I idolized my father. And the pedestal I placed him on climbed higher with each passing year. In fact, everything I did and everywhere I went, the notion of being just like my father was never far from my thoughts. My earliest memories were filled with, more than anything else, wanting to live and behave like my dad.

What was there not to love about the man? He was a gregarious, loving father and a WWII veteran. He fought in the Korean War and was wounded in the line of duty, receiving a medal for bravery in battle. After returning from that conflict he became a successful businessman. And to me, there was no more noble way to die than to give your life to save someone else. And my dad did so protecting a helpless, battered housewife.

In short, my dad had known the chaos of the battlefield and had so risen to the occasion he was decorated with one of the greatest honors a soldier could receive: a Purple Heart. And he carried this same sense of enthusiasm and heroism into the business world. He may have died, but in the mind of an impressionable, developing child, he was a hero in every way.

It would come as no surprise to tell you that my mother, older brother and sisters often told me that I was my father's, "little man." In fact, I emulated my dad to the point that I could often be seen walking around the house with one of his unlit cigar butts in my mouth. I was just 3-years-old.

From early childhood on, whenever someone asked about my dad, I would speak of him as a heroic man who served his country and died protecting a defenseless woman. So great was the influence that my dad had on me that as a child I often had dreams about him clad in his battle fatigues returning home as a conquering war hero.

The pedestal I put my dad on and my solid as stone image of him upon it was so high it was as if it lived in the rarified air of the highest mountain. It was fortified by unscaleable, impenetrable walls of love and wrapped in a thick shroud of undeniable hero worship. The older I got, the more impenetrable the fortress and the more layers his life and reputation were wound in. I was thoroughly convinced that no son could admire a deceased father more than I did mine. But the fortress would fall; suffering a catastrophic, fatal blow from the truth.

It was Thanksgiving Day 1980 and our family had gathered at my uncle's home to spend the day together as we had so many times. I was about 18. As was also our routine, we sat in the family room stuffed after an early dinner. It was then that my uncle made a comment about my dad that didn't fit the image of him that I had so carefully crafted in my heart. I don't recall what the comment was. I only know it didn't make sense given all I had heard about my dad over the years.

When I asked my uncle to clarify his comment, he took me quietly aside and said, "You know Larry, it's about time you learned the truth about your dad." What my uncle told me next was unthinkable; impossible for me to wrap my mind around. My father was not killed while protecting a woman from an abusive husband. An angry husband shot my father to death because he was having an adulteress affair with the man's wife.

In the high, thin air the walls of the fortress I'd built crumbled away and the thick shroud of admiration and hero worship was violently rent. My dad's pedestal fell away beneath him, and the rock solid image I had of him plummeted toward impact with reality. When the two collided violently head on, the image I had of my dad as a hero was obliterated into a pile of unrecognizable rubble.

When the love and hero worship was cleared away, I quickly poured the foundation of another emotional Fort Knox and erected a structure of hatred and loathing for my father. In no time I developed a deep-seated hatred of him. He was no hero, but a coward. Obviously he was unwilling to work on his marriage; he had an affair and got killed as a result.

My dad, the person who should have compassionately taught me so many life lessons and loved me, cheated me out of the years I should have had with a father; the one parent who should have fished and played ball with me. I didn't care if he'd been wounded in battle or if he'd saved one or even a hundred men. He'd purposely cheated me out of the life I deserved.

I soon realized that I wasn't the only one who suffered. His death must have been particularly devastating for my mother. If there's a worse way to lose a spouse than at the hands of a husband whose wife was having an affair with your spouse, I can't think of one. The grief from losing a spouse is far more than some of the strongest of individuals can bear, yet she had to deal with the shame and embarrassment of a husband who was unfaithful and killed because of it.

What made the grief even more difficult for my mother to bear was that she was madly in love with my father—my brother had often told me this over the years. I figured that the loss of her spouse and the betrayal of their marriage by the man that mattered most led her to abuse alcohol so that she didn't have to deal with her feelings. It forced my mother into a drug-induced state that it would take her years to recover from.

It was as if my father's affair and his resulting death set off a powerful explosion in our family. And no one escaped the damage. I went from a happy-go-lucky kid to an adult so filled with hate for my father that it seemed to be oozing out of every pore in my body. Of course, my brother and sisters had to cope with the grief and embarrassment of what my father had done as well.

What I'm trying to say is that I blamed my dad for my mom's abuse of alcohol and how it ruled her and our home. It was clear that my father was responsible for every difficulty we faced as a family, from my mother's alcoholism to all of us kids feeling just plain lonely because we were fatherless. As time went on, even after I came to accept Christ, my hatred and intense bitterness grew for this man who had abandoned us to satisfy his own selfish desires.

I'll skip a lot of the details at this point, but there was an evening in 1999 when I went before the elders of my church. I did so because of the resurgence of my tremendous fear of death and nothingness that had plagued me prior to becoming a Christian (see "Larry's Anguish"). I met with the elders and told them about the spiritual demons that were threatening my faith. As a result we talked, read Scripture and all of them prayed fervently for me.

As they interceded, I could feel the comfort of the Holy Spirit relieving my fears and reminding me of God's presence in my life. As I was walking out the door that evening one of the pastors stopped me and asked me a simple question that was more loaded than a shack full of 4th of July fireworks. "Larry," he said, "how are things between you and your dad?"

If looks could kill, that pastor's heart would've stopped beating that instant. Such was the glance I threw him. "He's dead," I said abruptly, the hate in my voice obvious to anyone within earshot. "And I hope he's burning in hell!"

Before I could leave another pastor grabbed me and said, "Hold on Larry, I think we have some other issues that we need to discuss."

The next morning I began a 13-week study of God's word along with two pastors from our church, Randy Murphy and Joel Mishler. This study, "Called to Obedience," took me through a period of spiritual growth like I had never experienced up to that point in my walk with Christ. It was through the study of God's word and accountability to two godly men in my life that allowed me to ultimately forgive my father.

God showed me that my dad was a man and a sinner just like me. He revealed that my bitterness and unforgiveness had not only affected my relationship with my earthly father, but it was also limiting my relationship with my Heavenly Father.

Today, although I sometimes wonder what it would have been like to grow up with a normal dad that gave me love, direction and spent time with me, I can honestly say that I no longer hate my father. I have forgiven him. And in doing so, I can now talk about him realistically as a man with good qualities worthy of admiring, and foibles that made him less than perfect. I even lovingly display pictures of him in my home and office, something I had never done before.

Most important of all, my relationship with my Heavenly Father has been strengthened because of the process I went through to forgive my dad. And God, by his grace, has allowed me to know him more intimately, increased my desire to walk close to him, and keep a tight grip on my Abba Father's hand. Finally, he promised me that in this life or the next, *He* will never let go.

6. The Tool of HUMILITY

Tool Verses:

Philippians 2:8 "And being found in appearance as a man, he humbled himself and became obedient to death even death on a cross!"

James 4:6: "But he gives us more grace. That is why Scripture says: 'God opposes the proud but gives grace to the humble.'"

Matthew 11:29 "Take my yoke upon you and learn from me, for I am gentle and humble in heart, and you will find rest for your souls."

Luke 18:14 "I tell you that this man, rather than the other, went home justified before God. For everyone who exalts himself will be humbled, and he who humbles himself will be exalted."

The Master Carpenter's Use of the Tool:

It is safe to say that no one has ever known anything close to the humility Christ experienced when he chose to leave the glories of heaven to come to earth. And live in a spiritual culture that ignored the state of a person's heart and among a people held captive by outsiders in their own land. From a human perspective, it is hard to comprehend why God would come into the world as a baby in the most meager of circumstances, and grow up amongst those he knew would take his life.

He could just have easily come in glory as the Messiah with 10,000 angels at his side, used his holy army to free God's chosen people from the Romans, and set up his eternal kingdom in Jerusalem. The Jews would have easily understood such an event and welcomed him with cheers and adulation fit for the God they had worshiped for thousands of years.

Again, Jesus made it obvious that the tool of humility was important to him by his actions. In chapter 13 of John, Jesus teaches that to be the greatest in his kingdom, one must be a servant, and he demonstrated this by humbly washing the feet of each disciple in the upper room. This was a common practice in biblical times usually carried out by the person hosting a meal. Yet here was our Lord, Creator of the universe and everything in it, bowing before an odd lot of men and serving *them*. Amazing.

Another incident where Jesus showed his mastery of humility was when he stood before Pontius Pilate. After listening to the ruler pontificate about who others claimed he (Jesus) was and questioning his identity, the Lord humbled himself before a man overstuffed with his own self-importance and said nothing in response.

It is a moment that has been captured on film many times…and always leaves me wishing Christ would have raised his voice, knit his brow, and made the foundations of the buildings around him quake in fear when he thundered, "I am Jesus, the Christ, the Savior of world and the Redeemer spoken of in the Old Testament. You have no jurisdiction over this small patch of desert, let alone the Creator of the universe!" My hope was that he would then manifest his glory, leaving Pilate and everyone in attendance so awed by his holiness that they would drop to their knees, worship and accept him for who he truly was and is.

Of course, that never happened because Christ knew why he came. He knew full well where his road would take him, and would humbly fulfill his purpose on the cross despite all the temptations and obstacles that were uniquely his as the Son of God.

Philippians 2:5–11 captures this idea very well:

> "Your attitude should be the same as that of Christ Jesus:
> *Who being in very nature God,*
> *did not consider equality with God*
> *something to be grasped,*
> *but made himself nothing,*

taking the very nature of a servant,
being made in human likeness.
And being found in appearance as a man,
he humbled himself
and became obedient to death
even death on a cross!
Therefore God exalted him to the highest place
and gave him the name that is above every name,
that at the name of Jesus every knee should bow,
in heaven and on earth and under the earth,
and every tongue confess that Jesus Christ is Lord,
to the Glory of God the Father."

As His Apprentices:

1 Peter 5:5 "Young men, in the same way be submissive to those who are older. All of you clothe yourselves with humility toward one another, because, 'God opposes the proud but gives grace to the humble.'"

James 4:10 "Humble yourselves before the Lord, and he will lift you up."

Ephesians 4:2 "Be completely humble and gentle; be patient, bearing with one another in love."

Commentary:

If humility was a disease in our society, very few if any people would catch it, let alone die from it—especially those who have found fame through entertainment and sports. In fact, it could be argued that, like small pox, it might only exist in a pitre dish locked away in a dark, musty corner of some isolated government lab. That's because so few people that are famous are humble, except if they know Christ and realize that fame and fortune are, as Solomon exclaimed in the book of Ecclesiastes, "vanity, all is vanity" apart from a personal relationship with God.

Along with the materialism that is rampant in our society is the tendency to brag about the accumulation of wealth. Because, as we all know by now, one's ability to make money and possess things has a direct correlation to one's importance and value. In other words, this belief results in a misguided set of values that results in arrogance—the opposite of humility.

What was Christ saying about the significance of humility and how it should be demonstrated in our lives? I believe he was saying that humble people don't think less of themselves, they just don't think of themselves. When we pick up our cross we humble ourselves to the point of "dying to self" and live our lives to serve others using our unique spiritual gifts.

As our Lord himself put it in Matthew 23:11-12, "The greatest among you will be your servant. For whoever exalts himself will be humbled, and whoever humbles himself will be exalted."

Example of a Believer's Use of the Tool:

NOTE: The story below is based on a true story that was related to the congregation of our church during a sermon from our pastor John Politan, but rewritten for literary purposes by the authors of this book. In order to preserve the identity of those involved, no names are used. It is written in first person from the eyes of a pastor (not Mr. Politan).

It was a cool, spring Saturday morning in northern California at the small church I pastored. Like many houses of worship we'd advertised a "work day" in the Sunday bulletin and several members had come to help spruce up the landscaping, clean up the church offices and make minor repairs to our Sunday school classrooms.

I parked my car near my office door and tried to slip into the facility unnoticed to quickly grab a thick, heavy reference book I needed to finish off the sermon I had planned for the next day. I saw a number of our members outside raking leaves, cutting the lawn and pulling weeds. Others could be seen through the windows of classrooms or going in and out of them with garbage bags and tools.

After reaching my office and throwing my light jacket over a chair, I walked up to my shelves full of Bible reference books and commentaries. I slowly scanned the tomes for the one that would add the final touch to tomorrow's sermon. As I continued to peruse the shelves I heard a scratching noise that seemed to be coming from inside the bathroom just off my office.

My brow instinctively rose with curiosity as I walked to the bathroom door and swung it open. I entered to find a restroom filled with crisp pine scent and a small, middle-aged Asian gentleman down on his knees. He was scrubbing the floor with a good-sized brush and a bucket of suds at his side. I recognized this kind man from the pulpit and had seen him at a few church functions, but had never formally met him.

The man looked up suddenly as if caught off guard by my entrance. A warm smile crept across his lips, then softly and graciously while still kneeling said, "Good morning, pastor. I can certainly finish this later if you need to use the restroom." Though it's hard to describe, this man seemed as comfortable kneeling as I did praying. There was a positive, humble demeanor that filled this man and spilled over into the room.

"Oh, no," I said, probably looking like I was at least as caught off guard as he was. "I was just curious to see what was making the scratching noise in here. Please pardon my interruption." He nodded and smiled softly again.

"Well," I said, "I need to go home and finish preparing my sermon for tomorrow. Thanks so much for cleaning up the bathroom."

"Very well." said the gentleman. "I'll finish my work here, see you tomorrow pastor," and he went back to scrubbing the floor with such enthusiasm it was as if he was determined to make it shine with a luster that no one had ever seen before.

Later that afternoon I finished my sermon and rehearsed it enough so that I knew it was ready for delivery tomorrow morning. I flipped on the television as my wife called me to the table for dinner. I sat down not knowing this was a meal I would never forget. As I watched the news with my wife, I listened to the story of famous sports figure who was recovering from open-heart surgery.

Nice, I thought, nodding. Open heart surgery may seem routine, but the truth is the doctor still has to open up the chest cavity. And the operation can be tricky. The skills of the surgeon have to be immense, and he has to hold up for hours under those glaring lights in the operating room. As I dug into my dinner I concluded that they deserved the accolades they received and the high salaries. We put so much importance on the heart as the seat of our emotions and the physical center of our well-being. For an individual to give himself over to such a physician for heart surgery is the epitome of trust, especially when the patient has nothing to say about the procedure because anesthesia renders him unconscious.

As the reporter related the story, a photo of the surgeon was displayed on the television. I felt as if the entire shelf of reference books in my office had toppled onto me...I recognized the surgeon as the same man I had encountered that morning scrubbing the bathroom floor at my church. That a person who'd opened up dozens of people and operated on their hearts would be humble enough to use them to scrub a floor at a small church was far beyond my ability to fully comprehend or imagine.

7. The Tool of SACRIFICE

Tool Verses:

Hebrews: 10:12-14 "But when this priest (Jesus) had offered for all time one sacrifice for sins, he sat down at the right hand of God. Since that time he waits for his enemies to be made his footstool, because by one sacrifice he has been made perfect forever those who are being made holy."

Romans 12:1 "Therefore, I urge you, brothers, in view of God's mercy, to offer your bodies as living sacrifices, holy and pleasing to God—this is your spiritual act of worship."

Hebrews 10:10 "And by that will, we have been made holy through the sacrifice of the body of Jesus Christ once for all."

The Master Carpenter's Use of the Tool:

Jesus' use of this tool is obviously best exemplified by his sacrifice on the cross. What he did at Calvary was the very definition of sacrifice. He gave himself up so that he could take on the sins of mankind and provide a way of redemption for the people of this planet. He sacrificed himself for the greater good of all men and women everywhere, and for all of those yet to come.

What also must be pointed out is that Jesus gave himself humbly over to a system that reeked of injustice, and to the cross itself. In other words, he did not go to his crucifixion bragging about who he was, boasting of what he was about to do, and complaining about the level of his suffering. Rather, Jesus stood quietly before his accusers. He used the silence following the questions hurled at him as a means of showing their guilt and the pointlessness of their arguments about whom he was…and why he stood before them.

Imagine for a moment that you are among the chief priests who must determine the fate of what many people in your society perceive to be the Messiah they've waited centuries for. And that you sense he's gaining a foothold with the people you hold sway over. What would Christ's silence tell you?

Of course, silence usually can only mean one thing: guilty! But here is Jesus, completely innocent, not uttering a word in his defense because all of his actions (healing nearly every physical malady along with psychological ones, and many times over) spoke louder than any of his words ever could. It was an unfortunate reality of that time that one's religious and political standing as a chief priest mattered more than recognizing the true Savior had arrived.

As His Apprentices:

Ephesians 5:1–2 "Be imitators of God, therefore, as dearly loved children and live a life of love, just as Christ loved us and gave himself up for us as a fragrant offering and sacrifice to God."

Hebrews 13:16 "Do not neglect to do good and to share what you have, for such sacrifices are pleasing to God."

1 Peter 2:5 "…you yourselves like living stones are being built up as a spiritual house, to be a holy priesthood, to offer spiritual sacrifices acceptable to God through Jesus Christ."

Commentary:

Like the incomprehensible love that Christ had (and has) for each one of us that resulted in his dying on the cross, so also is the level of his sacrifice. In fact, he calls us to offer our bodies as "living sacrifices" to him during our existence so that others might know we are Christians. In short, we are to give up or sacrifice all we have; even our bodies as living sacrifices for the cause of Christ.

What Jesus did for us and what it cost is not something any of us will truly understand until we are with him in eternity. However, many human beings have made sacrifices that are difficult for us to understand as well. Soldiers have laid their lives down in times of war so that we can enjoy freedom. Mothers and fathers across the generations have sacrificed their dreams so that their children could achieve theirs. And birth moms have sacrificed the joy and wonder of watching their children grow up by allowing others to adopt them so they could have a better life (both authors have experienced the last of these—see story below).

Yes, the sacrifice our Lord made for each of us is hard to understand, but so are the sacrifices that individuals make for their country, their families, and their children on a daily basis.

Example of a Believer's Use of the Tool:

When my husband and I were married in 1995 we planned on adopting a child after our fifth wedding anniversary. After that day came and went, we set the wheels in motion and started a journey that would teach me many things. The most significant of which would come from a young mother who already had two children. But decided, because of her circumstances, that she would give us her third to raise as our own.

Almost anyone that goes through the adoption process will tell you that it's a precarious road filled with countless bumps and with just as many highs as lows. Ours certainly was all of that, but what I want to share is what occurred at the end of one journey and the beginning of another: the sacrifice our birth mother made for my husband and me in the hospital delivery room the day our daughter was born.

Several months before the day we came together at the hospital, our daughter's birth mother signed a consent form that explained how she wanted the birth process to be handled in terms of who would be present in the delivery room, where and with whom the baby would spend its first night, etc. This was done according to her wishes. It was a document we glanced at, but its implications did not fully sink in until we were in the delivery room.

The moment that our daughter was born and the umbilical cord cut, she was handed not to her birth mother, but was placed gently in my arms first so that my husband and I could enjoy our new daughter's first few moments of life. This teenage mother might have made some mistakes in her short lifetime, but what she did from our daughter's birth on, showed wisdom beyond her years, and sacrifices I would find hard to make under the best of circumstances.

After spending some time with our daughter in the delivery room, she was taken from us to be checked over. We were told that shortly thereafter she would be brought to the nursery where we could feed her. When we arrived at the nursery, we found her the only infant there. After the nurse swaddled her, my husband and I enjoyed feeding our little girl for the first time. I had never seen such a small, beautiful, delicate human that I loved so much and would do anything for. Yet realized this moment would not have been possible without the sacrifice of a young mother I hardly knew.

Just over eight years have come and gone since the day we first held our daughter in the delivery room, fed her in the nursery and made the long drive home from that small northern Arizona town to the bustling city of Phoenix. We have seen our daughter grow into a stunningly cute girl with wits and humor to match; a youngster who has brightened the lives of a couple who wanted so badly to adopt a child and invest their lives and love in her. And of course explain and demonstrate the love of our Lord to the daughter he chose for us.

It is easy, especially given the pace of life we lead, to forget what a teenage mother had the maturity to sacrifice for us on a spring afternoon in the middle of a storm-tossed life. But in quiet moments of reflection we look back on all that took place on that day and marvel at the tremendous joy that came out of such a great sacrifice.

Simply put, it has made us realize how truly blessed we are, and that we will never fully understand what Christ did for us on the cross.

8. The Tool of JOY

Tool Verses:

Hebrews 12:2 "Let us fix our eyes on Jesus, the author and perfecter of our faith, who for the joy set before him endured the cross, scorning its shame, and sat down at the right hand of the throne of God." *His joy was to bring salvation to us his church, his bride! (Italicized note added by authors).*

John 15:9–11 "As the Father has loved me, so have I loved you. Now remain in my love. If you obey my commands, you will remain in my love, just as I have obeyed my Father's commands and remain in his love. I have told you this so that my joy may be in you and that your joy may be complete"

The Master Carpenter's Use of the Tool:

As the first verse above points out, Jesus endured the cross because of his love for us. And because going to Calvary was his Father's will, he found joy in it, just as we do when we endure suffering for his sake. But Christ also knew that after he had died for the sins of the world he would experience joy because he accomplished what he set out to do: bring salvation to us his church, his bride. And afterwards would return to his Father in heaven.

In more practical terms, Christ must have felt great joy when he healed a person who had endured a lifetime with an affliction and saw the person beside themselves with happiness at their newfound freedom and dignity. This certainly was the case as John explains in his gospel how Jesus healed a man who was blind from birth, and who made a practice of begging near one of the entrances to Jericho.

After the man received his sight, witnesses could not agree if he was the same man they had seen begging near one of the entrances of the city. The man's joy must have been hard to contain. In fact, his enthusiasm was born out by his repeated claims that he had received his sight by following the instructions of a man unknown to him.

It's easy to imagine the eyelids of the disciples widening upon seeing the man's joy after his healing, with smiles bursting out on their faces. However, the healing quickly caught the attention of the Pharisees because Christ had performed the miracle on the Sabbath.

When the man that was healed was pulled in front of the Pharisees and questioned in John 9:13, his joy was probably still highly contagious. One can imagine the man glancing happily around the room, taking in all the subtle nuances of color that his failed eyes had robbed him of. The high priests asked him who had healed him and how he did it, but upon hearing the evidence they were divided. Some believed Jesus was from God while others weren't so sure.

Here's where the exchange gets real interesting. The formerly blind man's parents were sent for and the Pharisees even went so far as to ask them if the man standing beside him was their son, if he had been blind from birth, and asked them to explain his ability to see. They might as well have asked the father or mother where their *Blackberrys* were, it would have made far more sense than their questions about his son's new found ability to see and resultant jubilation.

The scene surely got even better when they again confronted the formerly blind man, saying to him, "Give glory to God. We know this man (Jesus) is a sinner." He then replies to them, certainly saying in joyful jubilee, "Whether he is a sinner or not, I don't know. One thing I do know. I was blind but now I see!"

What joy Christ must have felt and given to all of those who were brought to him and healed when, in that day, there was simply no hope of breaking free of disease or crippling infirmities. Yet, Jesus was able to carry that same joy to the cross, because, like the Tool of Peace to be explored next, it was not and is not, based on a believer's circumstances. The Tool of Joy, like the Tool of Peace, lives apart from whatever life can hurl at the modern Christian.

As His Apprentices:

James 1:2–4 "Consider it pure joy, my brothers, whenever you face trials of many kinds, because you know that the testing of your faith develops perseverance. Perseverance must finish its work so that you may be mature and complete, not lacking anything."

Romans 12:12 "Be joyful in hope, patient in affliction, faithful in prayer."

Commentary:

What is supposed to bring us joy in our modern America? We've explored a list earlier that includes the accumulation of wealth, which has been boiled down to the phrase, "We've got to keep up with the Jones's!" Yet, even when you have the biggest house with all the latest electronic gear, two or even three of the most expensive cars made in your garage, it still doesn't satisfy. The bottom line on joy in America is that it is conditional; solely based on what you possess. The more you own the more joy and happiness you are supposed to experience.

In contrast, when Christians follow God's will in their lives, they have joy apart from material things and life circumstances. Obviously that's because Jesus taught that joy is to be found in knowing and serving him and loving others as he loved us. And that we are to spend no time worrying about what we shall wear or eat, because God takes care of his children. Our joy is also due to the very fact the Christ faced the cross on our behalf.

The joy of the believer is best exemplified in times of crisis, as the stories below demonstrate. And which, in an America sold on happiness with conditional strings attached, most people find difficult to understand at best.

Examples of a Believer's Use of the Tool:

By the beginning of 1990 things were looking pretty good for my little family. I was about seven years into a business that I started from scratch when we moved to Phoenix in 1983. Our income had grown steadily each year and was at a very comfortable level. We had two beautiful daughters ages 7 and 4. It seemed too good to be true.

Roxana and I were very active in our local church. We were the children's ministry directors of an active and growing congregation and very involved in leading small groups in the men's ministry. We were also part of a prayer team.

The only real challenge we had in our business, besides normal management issues and just keeping it growing, was that we had one very important client. Even as much as my firm had increased its business, this client represented about 30% of our company's revenues.

We had also taken on some pretty significant expenses in order to properly serve this company. This meant that we had an unusual amount of exposure to risk if we were to lose the account. Simply put, we would experience a big drop in revenues, but not be able to reduce our expenses for some time due to the length of our commitments.

After careful consideration, I decided it was time to take on a partner to help grow the practice and reduce this risk. After considering several offers I decided on an older man who had been a partner in an East Coast office of a large national accounting firm. It all made perfect sense. He had considerable and diverse experience and incredible connections and a desire to build a solid local practice. He also had enough capital to help us get to the next level, which he contributed to the company in order to become a partner.

By the fall of 1990 it became clear that the partnership was a big mistake. We were really struggling. There were many things this man had lied about that made a huge difference in how we were doing. What I did not know at the time was that he was also stealing from the company by siphoning off funds into his own pocket. We were just barely getting by.

Then in December, just a few days before Christmas, I got the devastating news. My biggest client informed me that he had sold his business and would no longer need our services after the end of the year. I was crushed! How could I have allowed all of this to happen? We were surely going to be ruined. I tried to negotiate an exit from the business for my partner, but he would not hear of it.

While the situation was very stressful, I was handling it quite well emotionally and spiritually. My confidence and trust were firmly in the Lord. Whenever I began to feel overwhelmed, I would turn to the Lord and he would give me his peace and joy. But I still had much to learn.

One Sunday morning I woke up early and felt like I had a pile of bricks on my chest. The pressure was unbearable. I stumbled out of bed and made my way downstairs to our family room. As I lay across the couch I pleaded with God. "Give me your peace, Lord, or take me home," I said. I really didn't care which one he chose. I knew my family would be fine financially because I had plenty of life insurance.

After a short time, I felt an incredible presence of God. His peace and joy came upon me. I began to see that I was looking at the wrong thing. My focus had been on the trial and overcoming it with God's help. I now understood that God did not want to help me make it through the trial, he wanted to transform me using the experience of the trial. The book of James tells that we are to, "Consider it pure joy, my brothers, when you face trials of many kinds, because you know that the testing of your faith develops perseverance. Perseverance must finish its work so that you may be mature and complete, not lacking anything." James 1:2–4

The truth is that the business did fail. Now came the worst part: telling my wife what had happened. I was never more nervous in my life. I felt like a complete failure. I had betrayed her confidence and let my little girls down by making such stupid decisions that put us in a place where we could lose everything. I cannot even begin to express how low I felt.

The meeting with her did not go as I had expected. Roxana was so amazing! She told me that losing everything, if that happened, would not be the end of the world. She convinced me that she still believed in me, and that I could do anything I set my mind to. She reinforced and strengthened my faith by telling me that God would not forsake us.

My wife reminded me of all the reasons she loved me that had nothing to do with my business achievements, while at the same time convincing me that I was a huge success no matter what happened with our current situation. She expressed love and caring in a way that I had never experienced in my life.

I learned some great truths about the Lord and myself through that time. It took several years, but we built a business that is so much better than what we had. In terms of our marriage, the greatest thing that came out my failure was the unconditional love of my wife and the intimacy I experienced with her the weekend that I broke the bad news. We've had some very difficult years over the course of our marriage, but part of the reason we made it through them was due to my gratitude for what she did in my incredible time of need.

Through all of this I have learned to take joy in the person I became through that trial instead of just bearing with it until it was over. I began to look at the end result, rather than the process. Our circumstances did not change for quite some time, but I continued to feel the joy and peace only God can give. And it had nothing to do with our circumstances.

Finally, what I now know is that any time stress begins to build and tries to bring me down I simply need to remind myself that God is at work in my life. And rejoice over what he is doing in it. The joy that I experienced during that trial is beyond explanation and will be a reservoir of strength for whatever lies ahead.

January 2004 was one of the most emotionally devastating and trying times I've ever experienced. Through the years since then, my thoughts return often to those difficult days and still fill me with fear. Even though no one in my family ever had cancer, I had a premonition that someday "it" would be a part of my life. But I never stopped to think about how much of my life it might consume. So in spite of "knowing", I could never have imagined the emotional roller coaster ride it would take me on and what the results would be.

I'd found a small lump in my breast. For the two weeks before I received a diagnosis I repeatedly told myself, "It's cancer." Simply put, I was mentally determined to accept the inevitable. Then, on the day I was examined by my doctor, I heard him say, "I'm uncomfortable with what I'm feeling." He'd found what I did, a two centimeter lump. After numbing it, my physician made five attempts to insert a needle into the lump and extract fluid. When he wasn't successful, he removed a sample of tissue for the lab to test.

While waiting for lab results, an ultra sound and another mammogram were taken. At that stage in the process my mind was blank and my emotions had gone into hibernation; I was on autopilot. I numbly took directions like some half asleep robot, going from room to room as nurses and medical technicians turned me this way and that. In one room a radiologist explained the differences between my June 2003 mammogram and the new one he'd just seen. Toward the end of his medical monologue my doctor called asking if I was still with the radiologist. He had received tissue sample results…I was glad I was still on autopilot.

Two and half hours had passed since I'd left my doctor's office and began my trance-like walk through testing. My doctor arrived and the diagnosis was confirmed: I had ductal cancer in my right breast tissue and it was poorly differentiated. The reality! My premonition proved correct. I did indeed have it…CANCER.

It was if someone had suddenly hit the "off" switch on my autopilot. I felt an abrupt jolt as my emotions awoke from their slumber and the controls to them were thrown abruptly back into my hands before I was ready. Despite the fact that I'd prepared myself for this moment for two weeks and I knew for so long that this was my destiny, still I was in complete shock. Yes, this was the diagnosis I expected but had refused to let myself truly feel and fear. Warm, stinging tears of grief and despair piled up behind my eyelids, but I had to hold them back. I didn't want to come off autopilot and have to work through my emotions just yet, but it was too late. I could no longer remain in denial.

The doctor's lips were moving, but I couldn't fully grasp what he was saying. How could I hear anything above the thunderstorm of shock and disbelief I was feeling despite knowing all along? Questions poured from the tempest like giant raindrops: Do I have anyone here with me? Husband? Friend? What now? Surgery? Radiation? No radiation? Chemotherapy? Partial mastectomy? Total mastectomy?

Before the diagnosis had even begun to penetrate my reluctant consciousness, surgery was scheduled; just days away! X-rays and still more lab work were needed. By 2:00 PM on that frigid day in January I was told I was free to leave. But where could I go? There was no destination: no tunnel deep enough, no tropical island remote enough, no frozen, barren windswept tundra cold enough that would allow me to flee from the diagnosis I was given…and somehow had to accept.

More questions paraded loudly through my fear and disbelief: "Who do I tell?" "What should I say?" "How would people react?" "Would they love me anyway?" My mind was spinning and my thoughts were caught in the raging torrent. "How could I tell my husband, children, family, friends, co-workers, and clients I had cancer?" "How would they react to what many see as the deadliest diagnosis any human can receive?"

The time leading up to the surgery was stressful and difficult to bear. It was bitterly cold in West Des Moines, Iowa with record snowfall and several days of sub freezing temperatures. Despite the weather my brother Larry arrived the day before the surgery from Arizona to lend his support and be there for me. I walked into the dining room that night and overheard my husband and brother discussing finances and wills at the table. In a way that only Larry can pull off a joke in the midst of such dark circumstances he deadpanned, "Your husband has you dead already…"

The following morning, Feb. 4th, 2004 my husband, daughter, and brother accompanied me to the hospital. Shortly after we arrived the nurse came to deliver me to pre-op, but not before Larry asked if he could pray with me. As we bowed our heads I welcomed his prayer, love and support as did my daughter and the nurse. My husband walked away.

I felt a huge sense of relief after the operation when I was told that the surgeon was able to remove the cancer and save my breast. Two lymph nodes were also removed. Thankfully, I did not feel much pain, but further tests showed that I needed chemotherapy to be free of the disease.

Later that night I sat with my brother at the kitchen table, unaware that he had brought a Bible with him. He broke the silence. "Today I said a prayer with everyone again before your surgery." He went on to explain that his home church in Phoenix was praying for me. It meant more to me than I could express. It was as if a warm blanket of God's grace and mercy was wrapped around me and I experienced the miracle of love from people I didn't even know. It reminded me of Psalm 4:3, "Know that the Lord has set apart the godly for himself; the Lord will hear when I call to him."

A month after my first chemotherapy treatment my son, Grant, who was 12-years-old at the time, came running through the front door of our home. "Mom! Mom!" he yelled. "You have to let me go! Nate and Lucas are going and they will take me." He explained that some of his friends were going to church and wanted him to go along.

Since the diagnosis my son had become very concerned about me; asking me daily how I was doing. I knew my deteriorating health was affecting Grant negatively because there were so many things I could do for him that became impossible after the cancer struck. He needed to be free from his worry about my well-being and have a positive outlet in his life.

Grant returned from the Lutheran Church of Hope excited about a program called "PowerLife" that I had given him permission to attend on Wednesday nights. I knew it was what Grant needed. For that one night a week my son had a safe place to go, be with his peers and not worry about me. He would be sitting in a service where the Bible was taught and taking notes he'd hand in. I felt such joy because God had provided a wonderful place for my son where he could be with friends and learn about the Lord at the same time. But I still prayed for his safety.

I began attending services on Sunday nights to ensure that Grant was listening and understanding the messages. For weeks I listened to sermons that were obviously meant for me. During the services I found myself in tears and could feel the effects of the prayers that were being said for my recovery. I felt joy in the midst of my fear. I felt loved, supported and lifted up.

As the weeks went by and my health slowly improved I could feel the Holy Spirit working in my life. I had a tremendous desire to pray and know God better; a desire that grew. I wanted to know and trust Jesus Christ because my faith told me he could strengthen me. And through him I could do all things, even beat cancer.

On Wednesday evenings, while Grant attended PowerLife, I started attending the pastor's Bible study class. I didn't know it then, but the Lord was just beginning to open my heart to hear his Word. For months I sat alone, absorbing what I was being taught. At the time, I didn't know that I was on my journey to know the Lord as personal savior; that the healing of my heart had begun. Pain was being removed and God's word was becoming clearer to me.

While in the Bible study I heard of a class that introduces people to Christianity called "Alpha." As a young girl I remembered taking confirmation classes where I had memorized the books of the Bible and a few verses. But this was an opportunity to learn what it meant to be a Christian.

In Alpha I came to understand that being a Christian is really about having a personal relationship with God and that it happens on a daily basis. It isn't just about going to church on Sunday. I learned about sin, grace and forgiveness. I was taught that God the Father sent his son Jesus to die for my sins and that by receiving the free gift of salvation I could have a personal relationship with him.

My Dad had died many years ago when I was only 9-years-old. At the age of 48, through this class, God told me *he* is my everlasting Abba Father and he wanted me to know him as "Daddy." God worked on my heart and my attitude. In looking back I realized that God had been knocking on the door of my heart for many years.

In a moment of insight and spiritual reflection, I realized he was waiting for *me* to open the door and ask him to enter. I needed to turn everything over to him; trust in him completely to become the person that the Lord wanted me to be. As it says in Philippians 1:6, "…being confident in this, that he who began a good work in you will carry it on to completion until the day of Christ Jesus."

Since taking that Alpha class over four years ago I have hosted eight Alpha studies. Every time I have learned something new. One of the most important things I came to know was that I needed more Christians in my life. Toward that end I joined a beginner quilting class. The class I had heard about was called "Stitchin' Mission" and was being taught following Christian principles. It was being held at a nearby church and I invited my daughter-in-law to join me. At the first session we learned that a Christian woman from our church began teaching quilt making after reading "The Purpose Driven Life" by Rick Warren.

In my few years as a believer I've realized that sometimes things need to be cut away…just as when I was making a quilt I cut away the fabric I didn't need. As I layered a quilt top, batting, and a fabric backing to make a sandwich that will hold together to form a quilt, I created warmth. In the same way, knowing God is like feeling the warmth and fire of his love; feeling his Spirit inside us, filling us with his joy and peace in the midst of fear.

When I make quilts to give away, my prayer is that his Spirit will be felt by each person who is covered by them. And that they will feel the joy I knew during my battle with cancer. And how, despite my sickness, God somehow allowed me to function through and even thrive inside it.

Recently I found a letter from the owner of the company that employed me at the time of my illness. At that time I had turned my work life completely over to God. I had no other choice than to let him watch over me as I did my best to work and take care of customers. A paragraph from the letter reads:

With all the things on your mind, I couldn't help but notice (of course I put them in the computers every day) how your business is growing. I don't know if February was the best you ever had, but it was terrific. It was a lousy month overall for the company and for almost all of the sales people. You were one of only four to make goal, and you were 52% ahead of last year. That's remarkable at any time, but when you're fighting like you have been, it's more than remarkable.

We think of you and pray for you.

I will always be grateful that Grant, who brought encouragement into my life, led me to church with him. He makes me very proud and is a now youth leader in PowerLife. And I am thankful for Larry who gave me hope. But most of all I am thankful to God for the experience of cancer, through which I received Christ as my Lord and Savior and experienced joy in the middle of such catastrophic fear. Because of that experience I have turned all of my life over to him, walking and talking with him every day.

Looking back across those difficult days I can honestly say my Lord blessed me with breast cancer and I eventually experienced an unexplainable joy because of it. But it would take the passing of the ensuing years before I realized fully how that was possible, and that God had orchestrated those events for his purposes in my life.

9. The Tool of PEACE

Tool Verses:

John 16:33 "I have told you these things, so that in me you may have peace. In this world you will have trouble. But take heart! I have overcome the world."

Romans 8:6 "The mind of sinful man is death, but the mind controlled by the Spirit is life and peace…"

Romans 14:17–18 "For the kingdom of God is not a matter of eating and drinking, but of righteousness, peace and joy in the Holy Spirit…"

The Master Carpenter's Use of the Tool:

For Jesus and for all of us who believe in him, we can find peace in God's will. Christ was obedient to the will of the Father and it took him to Calvary—that is why he had peace in the midst of his death on the cross. An experience that was so horrendous that neither movies nor the most active imagination can do it justice.

He gave peace to those around him when he did miracles, freed them from their afflictions so that they were no longer at war with their deteriorating bodies. As noted earlier, this must have given our Lord not only great joy, but great peace to know that he had brought the suffering of so many to an end.

In Matthew 8:23–27, Christ showed that he could bring peace in another way; He had the power to bring tranquility to nature. These verses tell us, "And when he got into the boat (on the Sea of Galilee) his disciples followed him. And behold, there arose a great storm on the sea, so that the boat was being swamped by the waves; but he (Jesus) was asleep. And they went and woke him, saying, 'Save us, Lord; we are perishing!' And he said to them, 'Why are you afraid, O you of little faith?' Then he rose and rebuked the winds and the sea, and there was a great calm. And the men marveled, saying, "What sort of man is this, that even he wind and the sea obey him?"' ESV

Finally, consider that Christ had a complete "peace" throughout the road that took him to his death. There was no struggle within him. During each step along the path he knew that his Father was in control and never wavered in his commitment to bear the sins of mankind. We are called to that same level of peace in all of our struggles. We are to let the "peace of Christ" rule in our hearts, not the peace we attempt to manufacturer on our own!

As His Apprentices:

Colossians 3:15 "Let the peace of Christ rule in your hearts, since as members of one body you were called to peace…"

Romans 12:18 "If it is possible, as far as it depends on you, live at peace with everyone."

Commentary:

Peace. The very word conjures up the thought of laying on a soft as down blanket next to a babbling brook surrounded by a tall stand of pines, their scent on a cool breeze whispering through their branches. With eyes closed and miles between yourself, the big city and the technology that ensnares you, it's possible to relax and forget the stressors that nip daily at your heels.

As wonderful as this can be, the truth is that most of us cram ourselves into huge, traffic-congested cities with millions of fellow citizens when hundreds of square miles of wilderness beckon. City dwellers dream of living a simpler life in the country. But even when they do relocate, they find they've unpacked their personal baggage in a new town and residence. A change in scenery does not guarantee that peace will follow any more than you'll find it in the idyllic scene described above.

What we do know, as believers at least, is that peace is not a destination to be reached, but a free gift that each of us can receive by accepting Christ as personal Savior and Lord. If Jesus himself found peace while facing the most difficult circumstances any human has ever known, we can find it whether we live in an urban or rural setting, whether our debts are paid in full or if our house is in foreclosure and we are about to lose everything. The example of a believer's use of the tool in this section is living proof of that. Christ validates this promise in John 16:33 where he said, "I have told you these things, so that in me you may have peace. In this world you will have trouble. But take heart! I have overcome the world."

Example of a Believer's Use of the Tool:

If I had to describe my family, I'd have to say we're a typical one with three children: two rough and tumble boys ages 9 and 7 and the sweetest little girl you'll ever meet that's just one-year-old. However, this story is not about any of them, but rather our son Samuel that would be two if he was still alive. It was through his passing that we learned the true meaning of God's peace in the midst of a stress-filled, emotional firestorm.

At the beginning of 2004 my wife told me that she had a strong desire to add another child to our family. I have to admit my feelings did not mirror hers—not at first anyway. It was a struggle for my wife to wait for the Lord to change my mind. She prayed for me constantly, but it took over a year for God to bring my heart in line with hers.

In June of 2005 we started to pray together about having another child so that we would be sure this was the Lord's plan and not our selfish desire. Our prayer was that we would honor God, that this baby would come to know Christ, and live a life that would glorify him. In doing so we thought about a favorite verse in the Bible, Isaiah 55:8, "'For my thoughts are not your thoughts, nor are your ways my ways,' declares the Lord." By December 2005 we found out we were pregnant.

Six to eight weeks into the pregnancy my wife became gravely ill. The doctors diagnosed her with a condition called hyperemesis gravidarum. The best way to describe it is morning sickness magnified by 10 times. My wife dropped 20 pounds in 2 months because she was not able to hold down much food or water. This was only the beginning of what she went through. She ended up at Thunderbird Emergency in Phoenix where they hydrated her with fluids and gave her a pump that sent medicine into her system on a continuous basis.

A few weeks later during a regular doctor's visit, the doctor found a blood clot near the baby. We were told that the medical staff needed to keep a close eye on the baby due to this condition. During many subsequent visits to our physician, she began to notice other problems with Samuel. As each week went by we were given small pieces of a larger puzzle but didn't have a clear picture of what was wrong with our boy.

After several weeks the doctors finally gave us the last few pieces of the puzzle so that we had a complete picture of what our son was suffering from. It was a chromosomal abnormality; something having to do with our child's genes. Because of this we went to a specialist who told us what no parent wants to hear: our baby would die at anytime in the womb or shortly after birth. The shock left us emotionally stunned.

After we got the devastating news we experienced a kaleidoscope of emotion, from heartache to fear to outright anger. Fortunately, a couple had discipled us on how to deepen our walk with Christ. They pointed out that when trials come, we need to ask God for the strength and peace to walk through them. They would always ask us, "Is God enough?"

It was what I needed to hear at that moment because there were times when I would feel so enraged it seemed like I had been hit with a lightning bolt filled with anger. What I came to realize was that I was keeping the feelings of loss and sadness about losing my son inside and I needed to let them out. It was not easy, but I learned to do just that.

At one point the walk through this situation got so difficult…I remember vividly lying in bed next to my wife so paralyzed with fear that I could not get up. My wife and I cried until we couldn't shed another tear; our hearts were broken. We were broken. We realized we didn't have the strength to walk this road alone. We would have to depend solely and wholly on God. He would somehow give us the peace and the ability to survive the nightmare of losing our boy.

It was when we stopped trying to do it ourselves that we saw the power of Christ work through us and we felt the peace that only he can give. At this moment in our journey, 2 Corinthians 12:9 spoke to our hearts. It says, "'My grace is sufficient for you, for my power is made perfect in weakness.' Therefore I will boast all the more gladly about my weaknesses, so that Christ's power may rest on me."

The difficulties we faced didn't end with the news that we would lose our precious child. There were many painful decisions to make and we sought the counsel of family, friends and physicians. Some family members and doctors advised us to abort the baby. I couldn't understand why they piled even more stress on us when it took every ounce of emotional strength we had just to make it from day to day. If God had not walked with us on every step, that would have been the proverbial straw that broke the camel's back.

My wife and I prayerfully considered our options, but abortion was never a consideration. In the end and with help from the couple that discipled us, we decided to go forward with a normal childbirth. We felt strongly that it was God's will for us and that we needed to be obedient. When we thought about our decision to go ahead with the delivery, we found great comfort and peace in the Old Testament scripture Psalm 139:13-14, "For you created my inmost being; you knit me together in my mother's womb. I praise you because I am fearfully and wonderfully made…" If the Bible is true, (and it is) then our Samuel was never a mistake, but a blessing from the Lord.

At 2:00 AM on July 18th my wife went into full-blown labor. Knowing we had a short time together, I read Scripture to the baby in the womb so when he heard those words he would be comforted by his Savior in heaven.

God orchestrated the events like only our Creator could so that my wife was not in great pain and a doctor was available when needed for the birth. And those family and friends that supported our decision to go through with the birth had the time they needed to get to the hospital so that they we could be vulnerable and they could cry and support us at the same time. I should not have been amazed how everyone poured into the place, prayed for us, and filled an unusually difficult situation so full of love that everyone there was touched by God in a special way that I'm sure they'll never forget. Samuel, "Thumper" Romero, as he was known to our family, lived here on earth for just 47 minutes.

Having had time to look back, we can see that choosing to give birth to Samuel and go through this trial has given us a deeper love for Christ like we've never experienced before. We have a trust in God that he will take care of us always. I have a stronger love for my wife too. I cannot even begin to describe how much my love for her has grown after seeing how she faced this situation with such courage and faith in the Lord.

The two of us also have a deeper love for our other boys and our little girl because we realize fully how precious life is. The boys also grew tremendously from having to deal with this trial at such a young age. I know that on some level they understand that life is precious and that their faith grew, even though it will take some time for them to put their brother's death in perspective.

Another thing that resulted from this experience was that we dove into Scripture, teaching our children God is in control. This trial helped them to realize how deeply Jesus loves them and helped them understand what Christ did for all of us on the cross. Having experienced how painful it is to lose a son, it has given us a tiny glimpse of what God must have gone through in sending his son to earth to die for each of us.

Before we went through this horrendous trial we used to say God was in control. We thought we knew what that meant. Then we traveled a path and survived it because of God's love, grace and peace. You can only know that God is in control when events become too burdensome and you have no choice but to place your hand in his and walk by his side. Then it truly becomes real.

Today we are still growing from the loss of our beloved Samuel and pray that we finish the race so that it honors our Savior.

10. The Tool of PATIENCE

Tool Verses:

2 Peter 3:9 "The Lord is not slow in keeping his promise, as some understand slowness. He is patient with you, not wanting anyone to perish, but everyone to come to repentance."

Proverbs 19:11 "A man's wisdom gives him patience; it is to his glory to overlook an offense."

Luke 8:15 "As for that in the good soil, they are those who, hearing the word, hold it fast in an honest and good heart, and bear fruit with patience." ESV

The Master Carpenter's Use of the Tool:

Of course, Jesus demonstrated patience in countless ways during his ministry. A great example of how the Master Carpenter used this tool is exemplified in the way he reacted when the woman caught in adultery was brought to him.

In this classic biblical account as told in the gospel of John, an angry mob rushes Jesus with a woman caught in the very act of adultery and demands swift retribution because of the wrong she has committed according to Old Testament law. They seek only vindication that will justify their merciless act of stoning, and to catch Jesus teaching heresy so that they might entrap him. In other words, the crowd is impatient and wants justice metered out immediately; they expected a quick response from this teacher.

As a witness to this spectacle, one probably saw a throng of people angrily churning up dust as they marched sternly forward, approaching Jesus with vengeance thick enough to cut with a knife. Suddenly, a woman, covering her face in shame and visibly shaking because she knows her fate, is shoved forward and falls to the ground in front of the Son of God. The accusation of adultery is delivered like a piercing sword sent straight to the transgressor's heart.

The pack falls suddenly silent, every man leaning ever so slightly forward in anticipation of hearing the pronouncement of death by stoning from the teacher. In that same moment, the woman gasps and instinctively protects her head with her arms—she knows her final sentence is about to be carried out.

Christ could have quickly told the group of accusers his decision. But instead, as the Bible tells us, he slowly knelt and patiently began writing something in the soil at his feet. Of course, no one knows if he drew a symbol of some kind or a quote from the Old Testament, but clearly this would have stirred the crowd.

Some probably began to stare at each other in disbelief as the silence became more deafening with each passing second. Some may have thought Jesus was stumped and had no answer, smiling wryly at the prospect of entrapping him. Most members of the crowd probably shrugged their shoulders and exchanged hateful, confused glances as a means of expressing their inability to understand what Jesus was doing. They probably thought something like, "We've brought this woman before him, accused her of a sin she is obviously guilty of…and he draws in the dirt?"

After demonstrating great calmness in the face of a demanding, hateful crowd, Jesus states, "Let the one who is without sin cast the first stone." It is as if the air of vengeance quickly gushed out of the crowd's balloon, the oldest and wisest members of the mob leaving first as they soon realized that they'd sinned countless times, and despite the wisdom of their years, were not perfect. This thinning of the crowd continued until even the youngest walked begrudgingly away, convicted not only by Christ's words, but by the actions of their elders.

It is here Christ asks the woman, "Where are your accusers?" She responds by saying she has none. This is where Christ demonstrates not only patience, but shows the depths of his love for this and every sinner when he says, "Then go, and sin no more."

Finally, in using this tool, Jesus demonstrates patience in two ways: with the demands of a mob bent on using their traditional laws both to entrap him and as a means of applying justice without mercy or forgiveness. He also shows patience with the woman despite the sin she had committed, suggesting that she live her life differently because of this encounter.

As His Apprentices:

1 Thess 5:14 "And we urge you, brothers, warn those who are idle, encourage the timid, help the weak, be patient with everyone."

Colossians 3:12 "Put on then, as God's chosen ones, holy and beloved, compassionate hearts, kindness, humility, meekness, and patience…" ESV

Commentary:

As the Master Carpenter's modern day apprentices our sense of calmness or patience is under constant assault. From the moment we wake up we are battered by electronic devices that often fail us (ever had a cell phone drop a call? Had your hard drive crash?), bumper to bumper traffic that crawls at a snail's pace to and from stress bearing jobs, to families that often place greater demands on us than our workplace ever could.

In short, whenever you feel your "calmness" slipping away, your patience is under attack. Pull out this spiritual tool by praying for calmness and strength whenever you feel that your patience is being tested. And, as the example of a believer's use of the tool below shows, you need to be open to God's leading via the Holy Spirit as well.

It is important to note again that with every chance to exercise this spiritual tool comes the opportunity to choose a Tool of Sin; give in to the stressor that is battering your calmness and exude bitterness, anger and hatred. God has indeed given us a free will, leaving it up to us to choose the spiritual tool that will draw us closer to our Lord, or a tool of our sin nature that will pull us away from fellowship with him.

Remember, practice perfects the use of whatever tool that the Lord wants you to master. In short, as authors of this book, we've come to the conclusion that patience is a trait God yearns for us to use with great skill because it seems that it is tested daily. As modern believers, there is simply no way around, under, through or over the fact that we need to work toward mastering this one.

Examples of a Believer's Use of the Tool:

I recall a time when Rhonda and I were remodeling our kitchen. Although the majority of the project went very well, the company that we originally purchased our new sink, faucet and other items from wasn't what I'd call "customer service oriented."

To make a long story short, we ended up having to return nearly everything we purchased from them. When I took back the items and tried to get a refund, it was as if someone had ripped the cork out of the emotional bottle I'd stuffed all of my frustrations into during the remodel, and they rushed out. In addition to that, it wasn't that the customer service rep didn't want to give us our money back; it was as though he didn't know how!

I was returning the items to the store on a day that Rhonda and I were supposed to be at our son's recital. We were to be at the recital about an hour and a half from the time I walked into the store. The person who was helping me seemed liked he had no idea what he was doing. After the first 10 minutes of waiting I thought I was going to burst. I felt like saying, "Hey, what's the big idea. Haven't you ever done this before?!"

At that very moment it was like God said to me, "Hey, Larry, what's the big deal? Can't you see he's trying? Be patient, lighten up a little." It was like God just reached down and said, "It's time you learn to be patient." So I did my best to take the spiritual tool and try to get better at using it.

Another twenty minutes went by and I still didn't have my money back. I now had less than an hour to get home, pick up my wife and son and make it to the recital on time. And rush hour was just beginning. As I stood there I began to fidget and felt any sense of calmness I had left slipping away. I began thinking to myself, "Come on buddy, go find someone who knows what they're doing, I need to get going!" And then, another reminder from God, "Larry you will never master patience without practice."

Another ten minutes went by and I started to give in, nearly dropping the spiritual tool to the ground with an impatient thud. "Is this going to take much longer?" I asked, "I really need to get going."

As he handed me my refund he said, "Here you are sir."

I looked at him and said a heart felt, "Thank You."

"No, thank you sir," he replied, "I really appreciate you being so patient."

As I walked out of the store I felt the conviction of the Holy Spirit. The truth was, and most of the time is, that I don't want to be patient. I wanted so badly to pull out the sin tool and show the guy just who he was dealing with, insist on seeing the worker's manager, then blast both of them for their incompetence.

Yes, that would have been easy. Using a tool of sin usually is. It can even feel good to vent your anger on someone. The harder choice is to use a spiritual tool, but it's the best option because by depending on God for help, you will be drawn into a deeper relationship with him. And at the same in this case allow others to witness Christ in your life.

As I reached my car I knew I was going to have to deal with the overcrowded city streets at rush hour, would have to hurry home and frantically get ready for my son's recital. It was God's gentle reminder that patience is a spiritual

"Tool of the Cross." And that it was patience that allowed me to carry my cross for that moment.

Growing up, I always knew that someday I would marry and have kids. Well," someday" finally did arrive and I married my best friend. After being married for about 2 years, my husband and I started thinking about having a baby. We decided to go off of birth control and I knew that it would be just a matter of time before I was pregnant. I was convinced that it would happen soon!

I wanted so badly to be pregnant. In fact I wanted it so much that I stressed myself out physically to a point where my periods would actually come several days late. Of course, each time I was late I would run to the store and by a home pregnancy test kit. But every time the test came back negative.

How could this be? For so long we tried to avoid getting pregnant and now that we wanted a baby it wasn't happening. After about 6 months of trying to get pregnant, I finally went to the doctor and was told that it is not unusual for it to take up to a year. Okay I thought, we'll give it another six months. During that time we moved back home to Phoenix, AZ and the six month mark came and went and I still wasn't pregnant.

Each month was an emotional roller coaster; if I was a day or two late with my period I would be hopeful that I was pregnant. My hopes would be crushed with a negative test result or the start of my period. Another visit to another doctor in Phoenix would start us on a journey of fertility testing, drugs, and various procedures all in the hopes of achieving a pregnancy. After more than three years of being on this emotional roller coaster, I was ready to get off the ride.

Up until this time only a few family members and close friends knew of our struggle. To say it was hard for me would be an understatement. I didn't want to look at babies, or see pregnant women AND I especially didn't want to go to church on Mother's Day where all the moms would be recognized. I held our fertility struggle very close to my heart and prayed that God would bless us with a baby. But the blessing never came.

One evening my husband and I were attending a membership class that our church was having and we were supposed to introduce our self to the person next to us. I dreaded this because I just knew that the topic of kids would come up, and of course the gal in front of me would most definitely have a "quiver full." Then I would have to come up with a reason why I didn't have any kids, and so on. So I say "Hi", she introduces herself, asks if I have kids, which I say "no" to and then I know I am obligated to ask her if she has kids which I ask, and she excitedly says; "No, but my husband and I are hoping to adopt!" Adopt? Why hadn't I thought of that? That brief introduction would start me thinking about my true desires. Did I desire to be pregnant or to be a parent? Up to this point it was all about what I wanted, to be pregnant. I never thought to ask God, The Creator of Heaven and Earth, what he wanted.

After much soul-searching and prayer, I realized that I really wanted to be a parent and I decided that I would allow God to bless me however and whenever He chose to do this, whether it be through an adoption or a pregnancy and whether it be sooner or later, even if it was much later, I would depend on Him. You see, up until that time, I was trying to control the situation and I was relying mainly on medical technology and a doctor's expertise rather than relying on my awesome, amazing God. As soon as I released this burden to God, doors started to open. I met so many people that had been touched by adoption in some way or another. I also felt free to talk about my infertility struggles and to let people know of my desire to be a parent. The peace I experienced knowing that God was in control of the situation and not me or the doctors, helped me to patiently wait for His timing.

In less than a year (actually about 9 months, imagine that!) we were blessed with a beautiful baby boy (Trent) through the open adoption process. Three years after that, God blessed us again by allowing us to adopt another baby boy (Jared) and then on our thirteenth wedding anniversary, I found out I was pregnant and later our third son (Cameron) was born. God hears our prayers and gives us the desires of our heart when we trust, obey and wait patiently on Him!

11. The Tool of KINDNESS/GOODNESS/COMPASSION/GENTLENESS

Tool Verses:

2 Peter 1:5–7 "For this very reason, make every effort to add to your faith goodness; and to goodness, knowledge; and to knowledge, self-control; and to self-control, perseverance; and to perseverance, godliness; and to godliness, brotherly kindness; and to brotherly kindness, love."

2 Peter 1:3 "His divine power has given us everything we need for life and godliness through our knowledge of him who called us by his own glory and goodness."

The Master Carpenter's Use of the Tool:

The Lord demonstrated kindness in so many ways, but the miracles he did to heal those who were ill were, in our opinion, his best use of this tool. Of those, the healing of the leper is probably the most profound; because unlike others he healed, (the blind, the lame and the sick among them) these infirmities did not make these individuals social outcasts by every segment of their society.

Lepers, on the other hand, were confined to colonies of others who had the disease, and with no medical understanding of the malady, they were left to live a hopeless and painful existence until they died. That is until Christ came along. In Mark 1:40–45 we see the healing of the leper and his reaction to getting his life back. The Lord had been kind indeed.

In looking at compassion in the Lord's life, it is necessary to go back to the cross to find an example that outshines all of the others. As he hung there, body bruised, dying for the sins of the world, he had so much compassion that even in the indescribable pain of the moment, he thought not only of expressing his desire to the Father to forgive those who crucified him. But listened to the pleas of the thief next to him on a cross and made him a promise saying, "Today you will be with me in paradise."

One of the gentlest acts Jesus carried out during his ministry was when children came to the disciples expressing a desire to spend time with him. Of course, as Scripture tells us, the disciples forbade them from doing so. Primarily because children were not valued in that culture and his twelve followers felt his time could be better spent.

However, in Mark 10:14 Jesus says, "Let the little children come to me, and do not hinder them, for the kingdom of God belongs to such as these." This was the Lord seen at his gentlest. A sun-drenched scene that has been captured in many paintings and drawings, with children smiling and Christ laughing as he playfully hugs a couple of them lovingly in his arms. Again, he was breaking down barriers by his actions, stating that in his kingdom, children were on equal footing to everyone else. In fact, he continued in Mark 10:15 by saying, "I tell you the truth, anyone who will not receive the kingdom of God like a little child will never enter it."

Another example of the kindness and compassion of Christ comes from the cross. As Jesus hangs on the cross of Calvary, his body bloodied from the nails in his hands and feet and the crown of thorns embedded in his scalp, he looks down to see his mother Mary and his disciple John standing there looking up to him. Their faces painfully despairing, as their beloved Jesus gasps for breath. As described in John 19:25–27, he looks down at the two of them and knowing their despair, hopelessness and coming grief, he says to his mother, Mary, "Dear woman here is your son," and then he turns to his disciple John and says to him, "Here is your mother."

It's as if he is saying to them "I can't explain everything now, but I don't want either of you to feel alone. Love one another as mother and son, look after one another." Here Jesus is hanging on a Roman cross, bleeding, his body badly beaten, struggling for every breath and his thoughts are not for himself, but are instead for what others and his heart goes out to them for what they are experiencing because of *his* suffering.

As His Apprentices:

Ephesians 4:32 "Be kind and compassionate to one another, forgiving each other, just as in Christ God forgave you."

Philippians 4:5 "Let your gentleness be evident to all. The Lord is near."

Commentary:

Whether you are considering these four tools as one or looking at them individually, acts of kindness, goodness, compassion and gentleness do exist in our culture, and are easier to find than humility amongst today's crop of entertainers and celebrities. In fact, in recent years the media has taken to celebrating events that fall under these four headings.

Whether it's a customer in a convenience store who witnesses a robbery in progress and risks his life to make sure that no harm comes to the clerk. Or a person who adopts and cares for an abandoned or mistreated animal. And of course there are those compassionate people (often couples) who open their homes to the countless number of mistreated, abused or orphaned children in our society. We often hear about situations like these on the nightly news. And for some of us, such heroic actions may come as a surprise, and we often find ourselves wondering if we would summon the courage to do the same.

However, it seems though that these traits are becoming fewer and farther between. Experts have even taken to calling the generation just reaching adulthood amongst the most challenged when it comes to manners and etiquette. Further, these experts have concluded that our present day society is made up of people that have taken rudeness to unprecedented heights. Just listen to Howard Stern on satellite radio if you doubt this conclusion.

As Christians we may not be able to turn the tide of rudeness back from where it came, but we can make enough waves through Christ-like actions to make a noticeable ripple.

Example of a Believer's Use of the Tool:

Throughout her entire adulthood Kimberly Schmidt (better known as Kim) fleshed out the tools of kindness, goodness, gentleness and compassion in a very tangible way. Until her death in August of 2009, at just 46-years-old, she devoted her life to helping others. Besides raising four children and keeping a happy marriage going for over 26 years, she worked tirelessly to help women in crisis pregnancies. Her ministry at With Child, a family resource and pregnancy center, of which she was director for about 15 years, was characterized by gentleness and kindness and fueled by compassion.

Kim cherished her husband and her own children and she would drop everything to take a phone call from them regardless of how busy she was at the moment. But she also highly valued others' children, whether in or out of the womb. She did this by helping abortion-minded women realize what a poor choice they were about to make, but she didn't stop there. She either helped equip them for being a good parent or helped them find a loving Christian couple to care for the child. It gave Kim tremendous joy to hold a baby that would have otherwise been aborted and she was the happiest with babies piled all around her.

The manner in which Kim spoke with her clients was always gentle. She never judged anyone. But instead she always showed them understanding and empathy. Rather than preaching to them, as many zealous, well-meaning Christians would do, Kim challenged women in crisis through probing them with questions that would lead them to their own realization of what they truly wanted. It has been said that a woman wants an abortion as much as a fox wants to gnaw off its foot to free itself from a trap. Many women who knew no other choice but abortion came to Kim to help them understand fully what their options really were.

Kim's kindness was not limited to giving women counsel; she showed it in many other ways, for it was the very basis of her ministry. She not only helped women through their difficult decisions about whether to raise the child themselves or place for adoption, but helped them obtain prenatal care. She personally took them to doctors' appointments and coached countless women through labor. Through her grant writing and fund raising efforts she was able to use generous donations to With Child to give women who were financially strapped a variety of baby products: from formula and diapers to car seats and strollers.

No matter what background her clients were from Kim was eager to help. Many of those she served are seen as outcasts in our society, such as undocumented workers, preachers' daughters who became pregnant outside of marriage and girls who were forced into sexual relations by an older relative. Kim's heart bled for everyone, regardless of race (about half of her clients were Hispanic), occupation (even some erotic dancers and prostitutes) or background, whether addicted, abandoned or abused. Kim had compassion for those who experienced any one of these hardships as she had personally experienced many of them.

At a young age, Kim was exposed to illegal drugs and witnessed firsthand their ravaging effects on people. But, fortunately she never fell into addiction herself. After her adoptive father committed suicide, her mother went through a very tumultuous time in her life, and ended up abandoning all six of her children when Kim was 13. While under the care of her grandmother, Kim was raped when she was 14, but no charges were pressed. Adding to that pain was her miscarriage of the baby boy she had conceived by the rapist.

Fortunately, since she had accepted Christ as her Lord and Savior when she was 11-years-old and had a few loving Christian families take her under their wing during her teen years, these hardships did not break her spirit. Rather, they fueled her passion to help others facing similar challenges. She kept serving others in need, often to the point of exhaustion, even though she suffered from chronic pain for the last several years of her life.

There were times when she was taken advantage of by her clients because she trusted them implicitly so that they in turn would trust her enough to enable her to minister to them effectively. Though it hurt her deeply and discouraged her for a while, Kim was quick to jump back into her work, as she was convinced beyond a shadow of a doubt that she was doing exactly what God had called her to do.

In addition to addressing her clients' physical and emotional needs, Kim was always sure to address their spiritual needs as well. In sharing Christ with them, Kim's central theme was the unconditional love of the Father. For it is his love that attracted her to Christ and sustained her, as well as enabled her to be the kind, gentle and compassionate person she was—and will continue to be in glory.

12. The Tool of SELF-CONTROL

Tool Verses:

1 Peter 4:7 "...Therefore be clear minded and self-controlled so that you can pray."

1 Peter 5:8 "Be self-controlled and alert. Your enemy the devil prowls around like a roaring lion looking for someone to devour."

Proverbs 16:32 "Better a patient man than a warrior, a man who controls his temper than one who takes a city."

The Master Carpenter's Use of the Tool:

Given the limitless power Christ had at his disposal and how he was mocked, railroaded and crucified, the Son of God exercised a level of self-control that we can only imagine. In the gospel of Matthew chapter 27, verses 28–30 tell us his persecutors spit in his face. It seems that no matter the time period, the culture or the place, spitting in someone's face is the ultimate insult.

It often serves as a spark that touches off emotional dynamite in the victim resulting in an angry defensive outburst at the very least, and rage coupled with physical assault at worst. But this clearly was not the case with Jesus. And on some level, it must have mystified those who heaped this abuse upon him.

Unfortunately, they weren't done. The wall of abuse only had a couple layers of bricks. They added another when they struck him with their fists, another when others slapped him. Another layer was piled on top of that when they stripped Jesus, another when they put a scarlet robe on him, still another when they put a crown of thorns on his head, and another when they put a staff in his hand. The wall of sinful acts grew even higher when they taunted him by saying, "Hail King of the Jews!"

They spit on him again, adding more height to the wall. And it was finished when they took the staff and hit him repeatedly in the head and crucified him, adding a final layer of sin to the barrier between themselves and a loving, forgiving God; the Creator of the universe who stood in their very midst. This wall of sinful acts, now towering high, was held fast by the mortar of injustice. Yet, Christ would gladly have pulverized the bricks and mortar; forgotten who built it if his accusers repented and simply believed he was the Messiah.

Jesus knew what lie ahead of him prior to the scene described above. And his response when Peter drew his sword and cut off the ear of a Roman solider was a simple question that reveals self-control only the Son of the Living God could possess, "Do you think I cannot call on my Father, and he will at once put at my disposal more than twelve legions of angels?" Further, he could have issued the command to God, "Destroy them, let's show them who they're dealing with." But instead said, "Forgive them father for they know not what they do."

This is not only a scene resplendent with self-control, but one of kindness, goodness, compassion and gentleness. Christ obviously cared more about the salvation of those who were persecuting him than he did about his own life. A set of tools so powerful that his ability to use them coupled with God's strength allowed him to fulfill his destiny on the cross.

Any other person with any less self-control and such absolute power would have destroyed everything and everyone connected with such a miscarriage of justice...

As His Apprentices:

2 Peter 1:5–6 "For this very reason, make every effort to add to your faith, goodness; and to goodness, knowledge; and to knowledge, self-control; and to self-control..."

Romans 6:12 "Therefore do not let sin reign in your mortal body so that you obey its evil desires."

Ephesians 4:26–27 "In your anger do not sin: Do not let the sun go down while you are still angry, and do not give the devil a foothold."

Commentary:

Self-control? It seems to be a difficult a commodity to find in American culture. Cars have been around since the turn of the 20th century. "Road rage?" A recent development.

In case you've been holed up in a remote mountain cabin for the last decade, "road ragers," as they are now called, are individuals with so little self-control that if someone cuts them off in traffic they respond by running the offender off the road, smashing into them or both. Worse yet, some of these people have followed what they see as the "guilty" driver home, pulled a gun and murdered the person...for committing a snafu in traffic!

On a recent *Nightly News* broadcast on NBC, a reporter said that over the past decade there has been an encouraging and consistent drop in the crime rate. Yet, over the past year the rate of criminal offenses had spiked by 2.5%. Now that doesn't sound like much, but when it comes to the actual numbers behind that percentage, it's enough to worry law enforcement.

As one expert put it, "It's not enough to commit robbery. It seems that now if someone robs a place, he has to shoot someone too." These are the underpinnings, the symptoms of a loss of control in our culture. Said another person in law enforcement familiar with the rise in violent crime (and the loss of self-control at its roots), "If someone looks at a girl the wrong way, a gun is involved." It was easy to hear the resignation in the man's voice.

Yet there still seemed to be hope; a positive sense that somehow America's youth can find a way to resolve disputes with enough self-control that violent behavior would no longer be part of the equation.

Is there any hope that those who need self-control can attain it apart from a change in the heart? We as authors don't think so. And if you apply humanistic solutions only the symptoms are being treated and not the cause. It's like giving morphine to a patient with acute abdominal pain but ignoring the real problem: he needs an appendectomy!

Until our hearts or old nature is removed by accepting Christ, permanent change is not possible. And the same holds true for all of the spiritual tools: we cannot hope to use them on a consistent basis that results in permanent change without God's help.

Examples of a Believer's Use of the Tool:

As a Christian for over twenty years there is one particular area where I seem to fall into sin time and time again: ANGER! When I talk about anger, let me first say that I am not referring to righteous anger. Righteous anger is anger that is acceptable to God. Ephesians 4:26 says, "Be angry and do not sin…" Here, Paul is quoting David from Psalm 4:4. In essence we are given permission to be angry, but our anger must be righteous anger. Righteous anger is anger that is directed at sin itself. Righteous anger is not directed at a person (the sinner), but the sin. As we often hear, "Hate the sin, not the sinner." Hating what God hates, that is sin, is righteous anger.

However, the anger I have battled against is not righteous anger. Instead, it is the type of anger that manifests itself by yelling and throwing what I have come to refer to as "adult temper tantrums" when I don't get my way. This type of anger is the anger of man, and it is almost always self-centered. It is anger that is usually directed at someone or at some circumstance. In many cases my frustration (frustration is a nice word for anger) has been directed at my children, and I'm ashamed to admit that I have often yelled at them in anger. And although there were times when I became upset over something they had done wrong or when they were disobedient, too many times I became upset simply because they didn't do something they *should* have done. Or in the way I thought they should have done it. By the way, in neither case is this type of anger justified.

It has become crystal clear to me that the reason behind my anger is my own selfish desire to have things *my way*. Like a spoiled child I believed that if things didn't go the way I wanted them to I could yell and scream until they did! Well, at least when it came to dealings with my children.

I had somehow developed a mindset that because my sons were being raised in a Christian home, they should automatically act like "Christian" children. After all, they have been taught parental obedience in church, in the Christian school they have attended and *of course at home!* And by my definition of obedience that meant they should do what I said, when I said it, without any questions or discussion.

When that didn't happen I'd go into a tirade. After all, my children can quote Ephesians 6:1-3, chapter and verse: "Children, obey your parents in the Lord for this is right. Honor your father and mother—which is the first commandment with a promise—that it may go well with you and that you may enjoy long life on the earth."

They know the next verse as well: "Fathers do not exasperate your children, instead bring them up in the training and instruction of the Lord." It doesn't say, "Fathers yell at your children in anger when they are disobedient so that they will do what you tell them out of fear!" Now, I am not condoning disobedient children. The truth is our society has taken such a lax attitude toward disciplining children that it's not uncommon to watch parents and even grandparents being verbally abused in public by children who are barely old enough to speak.

As I have matured in my walk with Christ, God has steadily and faithfully helped me to consider my own sin(s) and how, on more occasions than I can count, I have been blatantly disobedient to him. What I'm saying is, that I like my sons, am a sinner too! But as an adult who is more versed in God's Word and God's Truth, he is continually working on me in this area of my walk. It is evident that as I train up my children in the Lord, he is also working to train me up IN HIM through my role as a father to three sons! By God's grace, he is molding me into a man, a father, and a husband who is more patient and self-controlled, rather than a man who is self-centered and angry.

Earlier in this section we asked if there is any hope that those who need self-control can attain it apart from a change in the heart. We believe the answer is "No" simply because any solution short of accepting Christ as Savior carries with it only temporary results.

You can call me "David" now. I am a real, red-blooded guy. My story begins when I was a young boy. I was exposed to pornography through my well-meaning "friends" and relatives. It started almost a 30-year journey of bondage, and lack of self-control. Now I am 42 and walk in freedom by God's grace.

Pornography was my tool to feed and satisfy lust, which never really could be satisfied. I spent countless hours worshiping at the lust altar with magazines, films, and photos filled with images designed by their producers to leave you wanting more. I exhibited a total lack of self-control.

During the times of indulging, the hours spent watching porn slipped by like minutes or even seconds, unnoticed. It was not uncommon for me to spend all night to 3–4 AM, or even 5 AM, sitting at the computer trying to see just one more picture or trying to catch just one more thrill before I call it enough. It never was enough. When my routine was over for the night, I felt so defeated. I felt totally out of control. How did this thing in my life ever gain such a strong grip on me? How did I allow this to take over me and lose my self-control?

As a born again believer in Christ, my courtship with pornographic lust always left me in a dark place. I could never reconcile the two, which always produced an inner conflict. After seeking ever elusive pornographic images and acting out, I followed this cycle of begging God for forgiveness, repenting, praying some more, and being OK for a few hours, days, weeks, months or even a few months in a row. But it kept coming back, like a bad habit hard to shake. On my own I was powerless and without self-control. Sure I had God on my side and shouldn't that be enough? Yes it should. But I did not trust him to satisfy ALL my needs, so I tried to help HIM out, by engaging in lust and out of control pursuit of self-gratification. I was all alone. A safe place to be, I thought. I was so wrong.

Like Samson from Israel's old history, I fought my battles here all alone. I did not let anyone in, nor did I let anything out. I lived a lie in hypocrisy. On the outside I was a pious follower of Jesus, on the inside I was in bondage, wounded, and bleeding to death, with nobody to come to my rescue. In this battle I deserted my platoon far away and there was no one to cover my back. No medic to patch me up. This almost cost me my life, my wife, my kids and my career. It definitely negatively affected my ALL relationships. I looked at people differently. I could not really look anyone in the eye, fearing that they will see some how the leftover reflection of dirty pictures in my eyes. I was in bondage, running.

The power of this sin is secrecy. The more I kept it secret, the stronger its grip became. I lived a double life. It was tiring, hard and very taxing to make sure I covered all my tracks. I also had to develop a good memory to ensure I keep straight all my rehearsed stories I would tell in case of a bust. If you think that living one life is hard, try living a double life, which was spinning out of control. Actually DO NOT try it. It does not work.

The power of this sin was broken when one October evening I called a men's group from a large local church. I went to their meeting and for the first time was able to share openly with a bunch of guys. This first meeting started a journey to regaining my self-control in this area of sexual temptation. I wasn't "healed" over night. I was however freed from the grips of its bondage, because my secret was out and I no longer was hiding it. That was a huge relief. Slowly I began to learn how to respond to and control situations that in the past put me in danger of falling to porn and giving in to lust. I did an online study, which hugely impacted me and set me on the right course to freedom (www.SettingCaptivesFREE.com).

By God's grace I was reconciled with my loving wife. God is the only healer. He has healed our relationship and made it stronger to the point of using us now to help other couples going through the same battles.

Unlike Samson, who lived all alone and fought his battles all alone, I decided to surround myself with great guys, my brothers-in-arms. They are the guys on whom I lean on when the temptations come, and they do come. This time however I don't fight this battle alone, like Samson did. I fight it as David, with his most trusted men and trained warriors. Self-control is great but in this fight you need others to cover your back.

Fighting till Christ comes,

David (formerly "Samson")

Chapter Seven

OVERVIEW AND CONCLUSION

Overview

The primary purpose of this book is to help Christians become more devoted followers of Jesus by learning to master the tools that Christ himself used during his ministry and to fulfill his purpose on the cross. It is our sincere hope that this book will serve that purpose as you prayerfully consider and apply what you've read.

This work began by examining some of the commonly held reasons why God chose the profession of carpentry for His Only Begotten Son. As authors, we offered some of our own explanations, the primary one being that through his daily exposure to the literal *Tools of the Cross*, Christ was constantly reminded of the agony he would experience at Golgotha, and had to depend upon God the Father daily to cope with it. And because of "being one with the Father," found the strength to become sin and give mankind the only way to experience God's love, grace, redemption and salvation.

As a result of prayerfully considering what Christ had to cope with when working with the wood, hammer and nails on daily basis, it has led us as authors and believers to more fully appreciate what he went through in the

119

years before and even during his ministry. And given this fact, and that he knew the details of his death, the indescribable depth of his love for each of us. Our hope is that you have experienced this appreciation as well.

The day-to-day reality of what Christ faced having been a carpenter in a small community, and what he was forced to confront when he called himself the "Son of God" was explored in the second chapter. In the former role, we concluded that despite the tools that served as daily reminders of his impending and horrific death, scripture makes it clear that…Christ was not focused on his impending death whatsoever. And the first and only time Jesus showed any form of "fear" or distress in his entire life was not about the physical pain he would endure, but the separation from his Father that caused him to sweat blood in Gethsemane.

Another truth laid bare in this part of the book was the fact that being known as "the carpenter's son" actually hindered many from believing Jesus was the promised Messiah. How difficult it must have been for the Lord to know he possessed the truth that would set his neighbors free. And for those he knew since childhood to reject him and his message simply because of his profession.

The principles discussed in the third chapter included the importance of understanding the events that led up to Christ's death, his full knowledge of what he would have to endure, and what we can learn as believers from how Jesus coped with the incredible set of circumstances he faced. This section concluded with this statement, "It may sound simple and trite, but we would find our lives far less stressful if we prayed more, worried less, and turned to God for help on not just a daily, but hourly and often moment to moment basis."

In chapter four we wrote about the crucifixion as a time when "Christ allowed the tools to be applied." He gave himself over to the cross despite the fact that he had the incomprehensible resources of the Creator of the universe at his disposal to stop his suffering at any point, to say nothing of not allowing it to happen at all.

We explained that there was a point when the literal *Tools of the Cross* and the spiritual *Tools of the Cross* were both displayed in such an unbelievable way by Jesus as he freely allowed the former to pierce his hands and feet. Yet, in this moment, Christ demonstrated the spiritual tools of love, obedience and trust in a way that no human ever has.

"The Anguish of Christ" was defined as the moment when Jesus faced the fear of separation from his Father as he prayed in Gethsemane. The Lord's anguish was used to point out that all believers experience difficulties, and both of us as authors gave examples of personal anguish from our own lives. Finally, we realize that everyone has his or her personal agonies to deal with or crosses to bear. And we hope that you have and will continue to find comfort in the fact that God has promised to take on our burdens if we simply hand them over to him.

Chapter five pointed out that all of us are separated from God. But that the difference between the Christian and non-Christian is that the believer's sins are forgiven while those who don't place their trust in Christ will, unfortunately, be separated from God for eternity. What was also a key in this chapter was the importance of staying in fellowship with God by dealing with sin as it happens.

Of course, within the confines of chapter six is the foundation of the book, as it contains a list and explanation of the spiritual *Tools of the Cross*. In this section, life application of the tools was emphasized and included appropriate scripture verses, how Jesus used each tool during his ministry, commentary on how contemporary American culture views the tool as well as an example or two of how present day believers have used each one in his or her life. As has been said before from many pulpits and in other books, this chapter is where the reader learns to use the spiritual tools or is "…where the spiritual rubber meets the road."

However, the principles herein would not be complete without pointing out the other significant spiritual tools, some more general and some just as specific as those mentioned in chapter six. For example, the Bible itself is the

Christian's "Spiritual Tool Chest," because it not only contains a blueprint for living, but each *Tool of the Cross* lies within its pages.

To paraphrase John Politan, a pastor of one of the authors of this work, *a Christian cannot be an effective tool for God's use if he or she is not studying the Bible on a consistent basis* (remember that when tempted in the desert by Satan, Jesus called on the word of God). In short, *you cannot do what you do not know.* To express it another way, we must read the Bible so that we know what Jesus would do, what the Bible says, and what tool the Lord would have us use.

The Word, it says in 2 Timothy 3:16, is for training in righteousness. And like we've said about all of the other tools, the only way they can be sharpened is through practice. Finally, in the first chapter of James it says we are to be a *"doer"* (emphasis added) of the Word and count it all joy to accomplish the will of God and his purposes for our lives.

Along with practicing with the tools above so that the believer can move toward mastery, it is important for every person that places his or her faith in Christ to realize that by becoming a child of God *you* become an implement that the Father uses to minister to and draw others unto Himself. Metaphorically then, each of us is a *Tool of the Cross* when we are filled with the Spirit much like when a hand is placed inside of a glove. The glove is only useful, according Pastor Randy Murphy, when it is "filled by a hand," i.e., we are the glove and the Holy Spirit is the hand. *And each one of us is a ready Tool of the Cross when the Spirit works through us.*

As important as it is to be used by God as a tool for his purposes on this planet, it is equally vital that we continue to grow in faith across our lifetime. What do we do to grow in Christ? First, as has been noted, we must read God's word on a consistent basis. Secondly, we need to pray or commune with God regularly. In Ephesians 6:18 we are told to "pray in all things" and to "pray in the spirit." We should be asking ourselves the following question when we roll out of bed each morning: "What would God want me to pray for today?"

Thirdly, in Hebrews 10:25, the scripture points out that if we are to mature in our faith we must worship corporately or with a church congregation. Along with this corporate worship is the essentiality of meeting in small groups. And for those more mature in the faith to mentor those who have spent less time walking with the Master Carpenter. This is our mission in making disciples of Christ. As Proverbs 27:17 says, "As iron sharpens iron, so one man sharpens another." And in the same vein, Titus 1:8 and Galatians 5:22-23 tell us to be self-disciplined in our faith and in the way we live our lives in the world. Fourth and finally, we are to witness to others by example, and to tell those in our sphere of influence about the love of Christ.

One of the central themes that we have communicated throughout this book is that each spiritual tool takes time to master. What we are saying is that this is a process of spiritual growth, which requires, according again to John Politan, four distinct areas that every believer needs to know about and understand. First and foremost, you must truly be born again or accept Christ as your personal Savior (if you have not asked Christ into your heart, please turn to and read "Out of the Carpentry Shop" in the back of this book). Secondly, you need to realize that growth takes time and that the tools will not be mastered in a week, a month, a year, or even a lifetime (after all, we will be perfected only when we are in heaven with the Lord). Third, as noted, we need to read God's word on a consistent basis so that it is written on our hearts and minds. Without doing so, as noted earlier, we can't know his will or the principles he desires us to live by. Fourth and finally, trials and tests are part of each believer's spiritual walk. By experiencing trials, our faith is both tested and strengthened.

That leads us to what we have come to call the "Spiritual Power Tool," otherwise known as *suffering*. It is referred to as a "Power Tool" because like the electric version of, for example, a drill, it's added clout or power in our lives causes our faith and trust in God to grow more quickly than it would otherwise. Whatever form pain, stress or sorrow takes in your life, the one sure thing is that suffering is not something any of us like, nor is it something any of us can avoid. However, it is what keeps us dependent on

God and increases our faith so that we will use the spiritual *Tools of the Cross* for his purposes.

The same was true of Jesus. In fact, it is because of what he experienced 2,000 years ago that the Lord knows about our pain, and is with us in it because he suffered and carried our sorrows. He uses our suffering—the trials we experience—not only to draw us closer to Himself, but once we get through them, to minister to others that are experiencing the same or similar difficulties (2 Corinthians 1:3–7).

Conclusion

The ultimate goal of being an apprentice and walking with the Master Carpenter is to deepen our relationship with him and draw others unto himself so that they, too, can have a personal relationship with Jesus Christ. The primary byproduct of walking with Christ and using the tools repeatedly is *wisdom*; understanding about the Christian life that we then can pass on to other apprentices that have not walked as long with the Lord or had as much practice with the *Tools of the Cross* as we have.

On the other end of the spiritual spectrum, those who have been Christians for decades seem to have such godliness about them. That is because they have far more experience or practice with each tool. And the most mature among us have learned to welcome suffering with joy because they know that whatever difficulties they must confront, God will be at their side. The end result is that they will be made more into the likeness of Christ. Each of us can learn a great deal from these "mature apprentices" and should have at least one such mentor in our lives. If you don't, we suggest that you pray that the Lord lead you to one.

Another important element to remember as this book concludes is that *it is only when all of the tools are used that the "final product" can be made*. For instance, to build a shed there are several tools that must be used: hammer, saw, nails, wood, level, plumb line, square, pencil, etc. It is only when we use all of the spiritual tools for the purpose for which they are designed that we can enjoy the finished product: a life filled with wisdom that exudes the fruits of the spirit, a strong witness for Christ, and a deepening walk with the Lord.

The book's focus, obviously, has been on the spiritual *Tools of the Cross* and how to apply them in our daily lives so that we grow spiritually and draw others to Christ. However, as this book draws to a close it is essential that we look at the three things a carpenter does in his work because it is tied so closely to what Christ does in each of our lives and to the larger picture of Jesus and the church.

First, he builds. Whether it is making a stool or putting up the framing for a house, a carpenter is always in the process of constructing something. In the same way, God is always at work in us because when we accepted Jesus as Savior we became, "a new creation in Christ" (2 Corinthians 5:17).

Second, the carpenter restores. A wood worker may come across a piece of furniture that is stressed and broken. Using his special skills and tools, he will tear down what is already there and restore it to its original condition, often making it better than it was when it was new. A hobby of one of the authors is restoring antique furniture. Sometimes in the process of restoring a piece of furniture it is necessary to take a piece apart and in some cases to take the finish off down to the bare wood. Then the restoration can begin.

God often works the same way with believers, allowing circumstances into their lives that strip away those things that they thought were most important, and leads them to realize that their relationship with Christ is all that matters. And when the broken and stressed are healed by the Lord, they are better than they were before.

Third, a carpenter reclaims. A master carpenter has the skill and vision to look at a pile of scrap lumber, take the pieces, and turn them into something functional and beautiful. Surely this is something Jesus was fully capable of doing when he worked wood for a living. God, with his love and redeeming strength, can take lives that seem beyond reclamation and make something beautiful and useful out of them. He sees us for what we can become; He sees us as perfected (Hebrews 10:14).

As you know, Jesus Christ, Savior of the world, spent the years before his ministry working as an unassuming carpenter. But before his purpose on earth was fulfilled, he would lead a ragged band of men and teach them to build his church. This wood worker, this humble, perfect human being, laid the foundation of the church through his death on the cross. This made him not just a Master Carpenter, but a Master Architect whose plan, through his own death, would lead to the redemption of mankind.

It is, therefore, a high calling and a privilege to use the same spiritual tools he did so that we can tell the world about his love, forgiveness and salvation. And at the same time, deepen our relationship with the Creator of the universe. We hope and pray that this book will inspire you to do both.

OUT OF THE CARPENTRY SHOP
from *God Came Near*

by Max Lucado

The heavy door creaked open on the hinges as he pushed it open. With a few strides he crossed the silent shop and opened the wooden shutters to a square shaft of sunshine that painted the box of daylight on the dirt floor.

He looked around the carpentry shop. He stood for a moment in the refuge of the little room that housed so many sweet memories. He balanced the hammer on his hand and ran his fingers across the sharp teeth of the saw. He stroked the smoothly worn wood of the sawhorse.

He had come to say goodbye. It was time for him to leave. Jesus had heard something that made him know it was time to go, so he came one last time to smell the sawdust and lumber. Life was peaceful here. Life was so safe in the carpenter's shop.

Here he had spent countless hours in contentment. On this dirt floor he had played as a toddler while his father had worked. Here Joseph taught him how to grip a hammer. And on this workbench he had built his first chair.

It must have been difficult to leave. After all, life as a carpenter wasn't bad. It wasn't bad at all! Business was good. The future was bright. His work was enjoyable. In Nazareth he was known only as "Jesus, the son of Joseph."

And you can be sure he was respected in the community—good with his hands. He had many friends, a favorite among the children, and he could tell a good joke and had the habit of filling the air with contagious laughter.

I wonder if he wanted to stay. "I could do a good job here in Nazareth, settle down, raise a family, be a civic leader." I wonder because I know he had already read the last chapter. He knew that the feet that would step out of the safe shadow of the carpenter's shop would not rest until they had been pierced and placed on a Roman cross.

You see he didn't have to go. It was his choice. He could have stayed. He could have ignored the call, or at least postponed it. He could have gone back to another era when society wasn't so volatile. When religion wasn't so stale, when people would listen better. He could have come back when crosses were out of style. But his heart wouldn't let him.

If there was any hesitation on the part of humanity it was overcome by the compassion of his divinity. His divinity heard the voices. His divinity heard the voices of the hopeless cries of the poor. The bitter accusations of the abandoned, the dangling despair of those who are trying to save themselves, and you can be sure of one thing. Among the voices that found their way into that carpenter's shop was your voice.

Your silent prayers uttered on tear-stained pillows were heard before they were said. Your deepest questions about death and eternity were answered before they were asked. And your direst need, your need for a Savior, was met before you ever sinned.

And not only did he hear you, he saw you. He saw your face-the same face that looked back in the mirror this morning he saw that day. He saw the face streaked with tears, he saw the face buried in shame, he saw the face contorted with questions, and he saw your face. And it was enough to break his heart.

And so he left. He left because of you. He laid his security down with his hammer. He hung his tranquility on the peg with his nail apron. He closed the window shutters on the sunshine of his youth and locked the door on the comfort and ease of anonymity. Since he could bear your sins more easily than he could bear the thought of your hopelessness, he chose to leave. And he chose to bring light into the world.

———————

As Max Lucado has so eloquently written above Christ could have ignored the call. But he chose not to and he did it for you. He did it so that you could accept him as personal Savior and know the joy and contentment of living inside of his will. As authors, we hope you will follow the steps below and ask him into your heart and life.

The first step in coming to the saving knowledge of Jesus Christ is to believe that he is exactly who he said he is: the Savior. Further, you need to believe that Jesus *is* the Way, the Truth and the Life and the Son of the Living God. Notice we didn't say, "…that Jesus *was* exactly who he said he *was*." Jesus still lives today, for just as certain that he was nailed to the cross and died there, he also rose from the grave and is seated at the right hand of God the Father in heaven.

However, just believing in Jesus Christ is not sufficient enough to live with him in eternity after you die. The Bible tells us that Satan and his demonic forces believe in Jesus "…and they shudder!" In addition to believing you must confess that Jesus is Lord and that you are a sinner and fall short of the glory of God. You must realize that it was your sin that actually put Jesus on the cross of Calvary. This is a very important step in the salvation process; God tells us that if we confess our sins, he is faithful and will forgive us of them.

Finally, you need to repent of your sins. That means turning away from sin and striving to live your life according to God's will. After doing so you need to ask God to forgive you of your sins and ask him to come in to your life as Lord and Savior. This confession of sin and acceptance of Jesus as Lord is the beginning of your walk with the Master Carpenter. Here is a sample prayer of salvation that encompasses both:

"Lord in heaven, I come before you at this moment as a condemned sinner. I realize that I have sinned against others and most importantly I have sinned against you. Lord, I ask you to forgive me of my sin and to come into my life as Lord and Savior. God, help me to walk with you and live my life according to your will and not my own. Help me Lord to know you more and grow in knowledge of your ways as I walk with you from this day forward until we meet in eternity. Thank you God for sending your son Jesus to die on the cross as payment for my sin. In Jesus' name. Amen."

If you followed the steps above and said this prayer or one similar to it, welcome to the family of God! We think it's important for you to know that just because you have accepted Christ as your Lord and Savior it doesn't mean that your life will be easy and without pain or sorrow. As we have said throughout this book, that's not what the Christian life is all about, nor is this why we encourage you to use the spiritual tools above.

It will be very important to not only walk with God, but also to find a Bible teaching church where you can grow in your relationship with God and with other believers. Bible study and association with other Christians is paramount to your growth as a new believer. If you need help locating a church or have questions or comments please contact us at http://www.toolsofthecross.com.

ABOUT THE AUTHORS

LARRY MATHIS

Larry Mathis was born in Phoenix, AZ in 1962. Larry was raised along with his older brother and five sisters by his single mother after his father died at the age of 37. Larry graduated from Arizona State University in 1984 and married his high school sweetheart, Rhonda a year later. Larry and Rhonda have three sons, Trent, Jared & Cameron.

As a CERTFIED FINANCIAL PLANNER™, professional, Larry currently operates a personal financial planning practice in Phoenix, AZ. He is the author of "Bridging the Financial Gap" and speaks throughout the U.S. on personal financial management.

Larry became a Christian in 1987 and has been a member of Northwest Community Church since 1989. He enjoys writing, singing, hunting, camping, and coaching kids baseball. Larry also serves as president for the board of directors at With Child, Ltd., a faith-based crisis pregnancy counseling service.

TODD DUFEK

Todd Dufek was born in Sturgeon Bay, Wisconsin in 1958 and moved to Lake Havasu City, Arizona in 1969. He graduated with distinction from Lake Havasu High School and attended Grand Canyon University where he received a B.A. in Behavioral Sciences while playing on the college golf team. He was the first golfer to be named to the NAIA All-American Golf Team and the first senior to receive the Student Scholar-Athlete Award for outstanding academic and athletic achievement.

He graduated from the Arizona State University School of Social Work in 1982 and spent four years in the field as a clinical social worker before taking a job in the golf industry as a locker room manager at the Arizona Biltmore Country Club in Phoenix, Arizona. After 12 years there he took the same position at The Country Club at DC Ranch in Scottsdale, Arizona, his present place of employment.

Todd began journaling in high school and attended a writer's camp in the early 1980's. Shortly after that he completed a two-year correspondence course learning how to write children's literature. In 2007 he published his first book entitled, "CYPRESS TREE ODYSSEY-Making Sense of Trials and Tests On and Off the Golf Course (www.yourodyssey.net, available at amazon.com)."

In 1998 Todd wrote his first book related to his profession as a locker room manager and wrote a second and third in 1999 and 2008 respectively. The books have been sold to over 500 golf clubs in nearly every region of the U.S. In 2002 he founded the Locker Room Managers Association (www.yourlrma.com) and has about 200 member clubs in 35 states and two foreign countries. In 2005 Larry Mathis approached Todd about writing what has become the non-fiction "TOOLS OF THE CROSS-Walking with the Master Carpenter," a book that took five years to complete.

Todd resides in Phoenix, Arizona with his wife and daughter.